GOT YOUR ANSWERS

THE 100 GREATEST SPORTS ARGUMENTS— SETTLED

ALSO BY MIKE GREENBERG AND HEMBO

Got Your Number

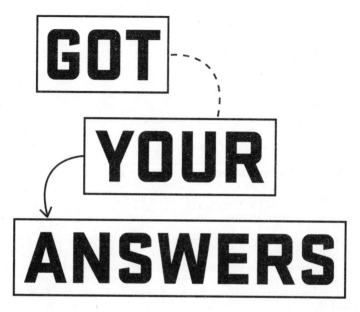

GOT YOUR ANSWERS

THE 100 GREATEST SPORTS ARGUMENTS— SETTLED

MIKE GREENBERG
WITH PAUL "HEMBO" HEMBEKIDES

HYPERION AVENUE

LOS ANGELES • NEW YORK

The authors would like to acknowledge Sports Reference, ESPN Stats & Information, and Greg Thompson of Hilldale Sports as invaluable resources for the research that went into this book.

First Edition, September 2024
10 9 8 7 6 5 4 3 2 1
FAC-004510-24192
Printed in the United States of America

This book is set in Museo Slab
Designed by Stephanie Sumulong

Library of Congress Control Number: 2024931172
ISBN 978-1-368-10858-4
Reinforced binding
www.HyperionAvenueBooks.com

SUSTAINABLE FORESTRY INITIATIVE

Certified Sourcing

www.forests.org
SFI-01681

Logo Applies to Text Stock Only

For Stacy, Nikki, and Stephen, as always,
for absolutely everything.

—Greeny

For my mother, Susan, who spent countless hours
on the bleachers watching me fall in love with sports.
Thank you for always being my loudest cheerleader.

—Hembo

INTRODUCTION

My parents were born two days apart. (Actually, they were born six years and two days apart, but the point is, their birthdays came two days apart.) Our family, as a result, always celebrated them as a single occasion—aka "their birthdays." What we usually did to celebrate was go for dinner to our special occasion restaurant, which was called Jim McMullen's, on the Upper East Side of Manhattan. In my perception, it was the most sophisticated, magical place in the world. Movie stars and ballplayers and heads of state ate there every night, people who were famous for things they had accomplished (as opposed to today, where people seem to be famous solely for being famous and often haven't accomplished anything at all).

I can still remember what the room looked like, and smelled like, and felt like; it felt important. When you were at Jim McMullen's, it felt like you were in the center of the universe.

So, it was February of 1978, and we were in the restaurant for the birthday celebration. I was ten, my brother was six, and our parents were each a year older than they'd been the week before. The room was electric, as it always was, noisy and brimming with energy. And then, all of a sudden, just like that, it went silent. Not a word was spoken from the booths in the dining room, the raucous laughter quieted in the bar, even the bustle in the kitchen slowed to a crawl. Time seemed to stand still, the air ceased to circulate, as though something so monumental had happened that it superseded breathing. Glancing around I saw that everyone, including my parents, had their eyes glued in the same direction, up toward the entrance; whatever was happening, it was happening up there.

Being so small, I hopped out of my chair and took a cautious step or two toward the center of the room, hoping to find out what this commotion of quiet was about. That was when I saw him. It was Howard Cosell, the living legend of sports broadcasting, arriving to have dinner with his wife. Now it was me who couldn't draw a breath. As a sports-obsessed kid, I took Howard Cosell to be the most important person in the world, and the reaction of the room suggested everyone else agreed. (That's not an exaggeration—in that moment it felt as though President Carter and Leonid Brezhnev, had they been, say, in a booth in the back of the restaurant, negotiating the end of the Cold War, would have agreed to pause a moment just to process the magnitude of Cosell's arrival.) I share this story because despite the fact that my mother will tell you I used to sit in front of the television when I was six years old and announce the football games, it was *that* moment that was the first time I can remember thinking I wanted to be a sports announcer.

The question is: What made Cosell so special? So consequential? He was hardly the *only* famous sportscaster of the time. Jim McKay and Vin Scully and Marv Albert were all among the greatest in the history of the industry, and they were at their peak in the '70s. And yet, if the three of them walked into Jim McMullen's naked and dragging a dead body, it wouldn't have caused nearly the stir that Cosell did. The answer to it all came from Howard himself. He knew that what separated him from any of them, or from anyone who had ever come before, was that he considered it his responsibility to *tell it like it is.* Before there was Stephen A. Smith, or *PTI*, or *Mike and the Mad Dog*, before anyone had ever even thought of being any of them, Howard Cosell figured out that if you offered sports fans passionate opinions, they would react. Some of them favorably, some quite the opposite. Howard Cosell may have been the most reviled person on television at the time, but everyone knew his name.

In a very roundabout way, that is how we arrive here—Hembo and I—with this book. Our first, titled *Got Your Number*, was a little bit about sports debate, but mostly it was about sports history. What made that book stand out, and what I am most proud of, was that even the most knowledgeable sports fan *learned* by reading it. Thanks to Hembo's unparalleled research, and my unquenchable fascination with the history of sports, that book was exactly the sort that I grew up reading. As a kid, there was nothing I loved more than reading books about sports history. However, what it was *not* was a book Howard Cosell would have written.

That's what *Got Your Answers* is.

We heard your feedback from *GYN* and took it to heart. You wanted more opinion, more debate, more declarative sports statements. Now you've got them. All of them. What you are about to read are the answers—definitive, unyielding, and unapologetic—to the one hundred most important questions in sports. You want to win every sports argument, every barstool brawl, every next-morning debate that you ever find yourself in? Now you will—because each and every answer is provided within the pages that follow. There is only one concern we share, and that is that once you are finished reading, there will be nothing left to argue about, ever again.

Please enjoy—and thank you, always, for all your support.

What Are the Top 10 Most Coveted "Trophies" in Sports?

Q: The United States has won the most gold medals in the Summer Olympics. Which country holds that distinction in the Winter Olympics?

1. Olympic Gold Medal
2. Green Jacket
3. Stanley Cup
4. Heisman Trophy
5. Tour de France Yellow Jersey
6. Basketball Net (Final Four)
7. Kentucky Derby Garland of Roses
8. Claret Jug
9. WWE Championship Belt
10. Gold Glove

Let's start off with a list where any of the first three could have been on top and I would be all right with it. Honestly, as one who loves golf slightly more than I love oxygen, my personal first choice would be the green jacket. Further, the additional perks the Masters champion receives—lifetime invitation to the tournament, a spot in the champions locker room, and the annual champions dinner—are superior to anything I have ever heard of elsewhere. The only thing that might approach those would be the one treasured day each member of an NHL championship team gets to spend with the Stanley Cup. Who among us has not imagined what we would do with that blessed day, perhaps the single best day any professional athlete could ever have? The trouble with that one is, it's only one day. The jacket doesn't have to be returned to Augusta National for one whole year. An Olympic Gold medal, however, is forever, and can be exhibited however one chooses for the rest of their life. It is the most universally recognizable symbol of athletic greatness anywhere on planet Earth—more than any ring or trophy or article of clothing. Those are the qualities that set the gold medal apart and give it the highest podium on this list.

A: Norway

What Are the Top 10 Dynasties in Major-Sports History?

Q: What were the only two teams to eliminate the Celtics from the playoffs during Bill Russell's thirteen seasons as a player (1957–69)?

1. Bill Russell's Celtics (11 titles from 1957–69)
2. Casey Stengel's Yankees (7 titles from 1949–58)
3. Vince Lombardi's Packers (5 titles from 1961–67)
4. Michael Jordan's Bulls (6 titles from 1991–98)
5. Jean Béliveau's Canadiens (10 titles from 1956–71)
6. The Steel Curtain (4 titles from 1974–79)
7. Showtime Lakers (5 titles from 1980–88)
8. Mike Bossy's Islanders (4 titles from 1980–83)
9. Joe Torre's Yankees (4 titles from 1996–2000)
10. Stephen Curry's Warriors (4 titles from 2015–22)

It is safe to assume we will never again see, in any professional sport, anything like what the Boston Celtics achieved between 1957 and 1969. Eleven championships in a thirteen-season span—including eight in a row—simply boggles the mind, regardless of the size of the league or the overall level of competition. My favorite thing about the Celtics dynasty is the manner in which it was constructed. Red Auerbach arrived in Boston in 1950 and began to build upon what had been a perennial loser in the NBA's earliest years. Initially, Auerbach had the opportunity to draft a point guard from Holy Cross but passed because he thought the guard was "too flashy." However, when that player became available in a dispersal draft (after his original team, the Chicago Stags, went bankrupt), Auerbach brought him in, and thus Bob Cousy became the first cornerstone of the Celtics dynasty. Then, after the 1956 season, Auerbach made a trade that netted Boston the second pick in the draft. The Rochester Royals had the first. The teams entered into a negotiation that included Boston's owner agreeing to send the Ice Capades to Rochester if the Royals would let Bill Russell slide to number two. Si Green from Duquesne wound up as the first selection. The Celtics got Russell, and the rest was history.

One further note: Hembo and I agonized over whether or not to include Tom Brady and Bill Belichick's Patriots on this list, and if so, where to place them. In the end, we decided that the teams they led to titles do not meet the typical definition of "dynasty," which is to say, Brady was literally the only player remaining from the early championship teams by the time they won their last. As such, they are not included here, despite the enormity of their mutual accomplishments, which you can rest assured will be well represented as we go on.

A: Hawks (1958 NBA Finals) and 76ers (1967 Eastern Division Finals)

What Are the Top 10 Individual Super Bowl Performances?

Q: Which player caught the last touchdown pass Tom Brady ever threw in a Super Bowl?

1. Tom Brady (LI) — 28–3 comeback
2. Jerry Rice (XXIII) — 215 Rec yds, TD
3. Terrell Davis (XXXII) — 157 Rush yds, 3 TD
4. John Riggins (XVII) — 166 Rush yds
5. L. C. Greenwood (X) — sacked Roger Staubach 4 times
6. Steve Young (XXIX) — 6 Pass TD
7. Phil Simms (XXI) — 22 of 25, 150.9 Passer rating
8. Mike Vrabel (XXXVIII) — 2 sacks, FF, TD
9. Desmond Howard (XXXI) — 244 return yards, 99-yard TD
10. Santonio Holmes (XLIII) — 9 Rec, 131 Yds, game-winning catch

If you could turn back time to February 5, 2017, at the moment when the game clock at NRG Stadium read 2:21 remaining in the first half of Super Bowl LI, you would never believe what was about to happen. Because at that moment, Tom Brady was lying in the dirt, flailing, having lunged at and missed Robert Alford as he returned an interception for an 82-yard touchdown. The Patriots trailed the Falcons 21–0 and appeared hopeless. Brady was thirty-nine years old, and the Pats had an heir apparent called Jimmy G. Brady looked like the past. Bear in mind: At that point Brady had won four titles—one fewer than Bart Starr and equal to Terry Bradshaw and Joe Montana. Otherwise put, his legacy as the greatest quarterback ever was by no means certain. Had it not been for that second-half comeback, he may well have finished his career with those four rings—leaving the rest of us to debate who belonged at the top of the heap. That night was not just the night the Pats won the Super Bowl, it was also the night Tom Brady became the GOAT.

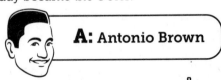

A: Antonio Brown

What Are the Top 10 NBA Finals MVP Performances?

Q: Which player owns the highest career scoring average in NBA Finals history (min. 10 games)?

1. Magic Johnson (1980)—21.5 PPG, 11.2 RPG, 8.7 APG as 20-year-old

2. Michael Jordan (1993)—Finals-record 4 straight 40-point games

3. LeBron James (2016)—Led series in Pts, Reb, Ast, Stl & Blk

4. Shaquille O'Neal (2000)—30-point double-double in all 6 games

5. Nikola Jokić (2023)—30.2 PPG on 58% FG, 14.0 RPG, 7.2 APG

6. Giannis Antetokounmpo (2021)—35.2 PPG on 62% FG, 50 Pts in Game 6

7. Moses Malone (1983)—25.8 PPG, 18.0 RPG in sweep

8. Larry Bird (1984)—27.4 PPG, 14.0 RPG, 3.6 APG

9. Kobe Bryant (2009)—32.4 PPG, 5.6 RPG, 7.4 APG

10. Jerry West (1969)—37.9 PPG, 4 40-point games in series loss

In the spring of 1979, Earvin "Magic" Johnson and Larry Bird put the Madness into March, with an NCAA Championship that remains, to this day, the most watched basketball game in American history. A year later, unimaginably, when Magic and Kareem Abdul-Jabbar led the Lakers into the NBA Finals against Julius Erving and the 76ers, most of the country (including me, at age twelve) could not watch the game live. It was broadcast on tape delay following the local evening news. I, of course, stayed up to watch it. All those folks who *didn't* missed what was the greatest performance in the storied career of one of the five best players that ever lived. With Kareem missing game six due to an injured ankle, the twenty-year-old rookie named Earvin jumped center to begin the game, and finished it with 42 points, 15 rebounds, 7 assists, and the first of his five NBA championships.

 A: Rick Barry (36.3 PPG)

What Are the Top 10 Most Indelible Baseball Statistics?

Q: Who owns the longest hit streak since Joe DiMaggio's 56-gamer in 1941?

1. 56—Joe DiMaggio's hit streak in 1941
2. 61—Roger Maris's home runs in 1961
3. 2,130—Lou Gehrig's consecutive games
4. 1.12—Bob Gibson's ERA in 1968
5. 3,000—Roberto Clemente's career hits
6. .406—Ted Williams's batting average in 1941
7. 511—Cy Young's career wins
8. 714—Babe Ruth's career home runs
9. 755—Hank Aaron's career home runs
10. 7—Nolan Ryan's career no-hitters

Iwanted to give DiMaggio the number 56 in *Got Your Number*. The trouble is, Lawrence Taylor wore number 56, and he is the greatest defensive player in NFL history. Transparently, there was a lot of that sort of horse trading in that book, and I make no apologies for it. But, somewhere in the deepest recesses of my soul, it still eats at me that Joltin' Joe wasn't 56. I believe the hit streak DiMaggio delivered in 1941 is the most beloved record in American sports, slightly ahead of Cal Ripken's consecutive games streak. (If you disagree, ask yourself, do you know how many games in a row he played? I didn't think so.) In the youth of practically every sports-loving kid in America for seventy years, the home run records were the most indelible. Everyone could recite them. Babe Ruth, 60; Roger Maris, 61. Ruth, 714; Henry Aaron 755. The real tragedy of the steroid era is the diminution of those numbers. But DiMaggio's hit streak remains pure, untainted, as perfect as the day it was set. That's what makes it the best record in all of sports. And why a nation still turns a lonely eye to it, and the legend who created it, nearly a century later.

 A: Pete Rose (44-game hit streak in 1978)

What Are the Top 5 Sports Comedy Sketches?

Q: Mike Ditka coached four (eventual) Hall of Fame defensive players as the Bears' head coach (1982–92). Who were those four players?

1. "Who's on First?" by Abbott and Costello
2. "Bill Swerski's Superfans" on *Saturday Night Live*
3. "15 Rounds" of Muhammad Ali by Billy Crystal
4. "Baseball vs. Football" by George Carlin
5. "East/West College Bowl" by Key and Peele

I absolutely love every one of these and, frankly, the *Key & Peele* bit still makes me laugh the hardest out of all of them. But, taken in order, the brilliance of Carlin, the genius of Crystal, and the societal relevance of the *SNL* sketches earn them each their higher places. At the top, meanwhile, there is zero room for debate. "Who's on First?" is among the seminal comedic routines in American history. *Time* magazine named it the best comedy sketch of the twentieth century. Jerry Seinfeld is among the routine's greatest fans, saying "I really wanted to imitate this show in my TV series." (Little-known fact: Seinfeld so admired the comedy duo that the middle name of the iconic character George Louis Costanza is an homage to Lou Costello.) (Another even lesser-known fact: On October 3, 1920, Allie Watt played one game at second base for the Washington Senators. So, for that one day, Watt was on second.) The routine was originated by Abbott and Costello in 1937, yet it remains every bit as relevant, brilliant, and flat-out hilarious today as it ever was.

A: Mike Singletary, Richard Dent, Dan Hampton, Steve McMichael

Who Are the Top 7 Athletes to Wear No. 7?

Q: Which team did John Elway and the Broncos beat in the AFC Championship game in the 1986, 1987, and 1989 seasons?

1. John Elway
2. Mickey Mantle
3. Cristiano Ronaldo
4. Tina Thompson
5. Phil Esposito
6. Iván Rodríguez
7. David Beckham

There was no decision we made in *Got Your Number* that resulted in more scrutiny or debate than awarding John Elway ownership of this number over Mickey Mantle. And, as a native New Yorker, and the son of two Bronx-born Yankees fanatics, I fully understand the blowback. Mantle was, as Bob Costas so eloquently said at the legendary Yankee's funeral, "a fragile hero to whom we had an emotional attachment so strong and lasting that it defied logic." The last thing I would ever wish to do is diminish the accomplishments of a player so revered and beloved. I fully acknowledge that more fans, to this day, associate the number with Mantle than with Elway. However, I also would posit that had Elway accomplished what he did in a Giants uniform, or Bears, or Packers, he would be viewed as football royalty. Instead, he resurrected a franchise in Denver that had only barely ever been erected to begin with. Elway was the first quarterback ever to lead his team to five Super Bowls, two of which he carried practically by himself; few teams have ever had less business playing in a game than the ones in which Elway single-handedly dragged the Broncos to the finish line. The simple truth is this: If you were to fashion a Mount Rushmore of Yankees legends, you could absolutely debate whether or not Mantle belongs. If doing the same for the Broncos, you might well be tempted to use four separate visages of Elway; his impact on that franchise was about as great as any player has ever had, anywhere, at any time.

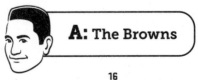

A: The Browns

Who Are the Top 8 Athletes to Wear No. 8?

Q: Who is the only player to score more points than Kobe Bryant's 16,866 during the 10 seasons he wore No. 8 (1997–2006)?

1. Kobe Bryant
2. Alex Ovechkin
3. Cal Ripken Jr.
4. Yogi Berra

5. Troy Aikman
6. Joe Morgan
7. Carl Yastrzemski
8. Steve Young

Time for some complete disclosure: The selection of Kobe Bryant for ownership of this number in *Got Your Number* was solely the result of the philosophical decision we made to be sure we found a way to include as many of the most revered athletes as we could in the book. After all, Kobe only played precisely half of his career wearing 8, and the other half 24. Otherwise put, we chose 8 for Kobe because he *needed* to be in the book, and Willie Mays needed to be 24; the exclusion of Mays would have been far more egregious than even that of Kobe, or practically anyone else. So, that was the rationale behind that decision. I continue to believe it was the right choice, and thus the ranking here is made in the interest of consistency. Clearly, were one *only* to consider a player's accomplishments wearing this jersey number, Ovechkin would deserve the top space. His achievements—by the time you are reading this—may include scoring more goals than any player who ever lived, and he scored every one of them wearing 8 on his back, a number he also sports when he skates for the Russian national team. (Hence his nickname "The Great Eight.") In the end, quite simply, the mark Kobe Bryant left on American sports is greater than that of Ovechkin, if only because the sport he played is so vastly more popular. Now that you understand the thinking behind the choice, we leave it to you to decide if we got this one right.

 A: Allen Iverson (19,115)

18

What Are the Top 10 Most Controversial Sports Scandals?

Q: Who was the "Black Sox" second baseman who made the Hall of Fame in its fourth class in 1939?

1. The Black Sox Scandal
2. Pete Rose Betting on Baseball
3. The Assault of Nancy Kerrigan (Tonya Harding)
4. Lance Armstrong's Doping
5. Steroids in Baseball (Before Congress)
6. Tim Donaghy Conspiring to Fix NBA Games
7. Astros Sign Stealing
8. Rosie Ruiz's Cheating in the 1980 Boston Marathon
9. 1972 Olympic Men's Basketball Final
10. Spygate/Deflategate

You already know everything there is to know about Pete Rose. Everyone does. Opinions on Rose vary. What there is *not* is dispute over the core fact that Rose bet on baseball. Shoeless Joe Jackson, meanwhile, very likely did not, yet he, too, remains in permanent exile. Jackson went to his grave denying any involvement in the scheme to throw the 1919 World Series. He hit .375 in the eight games (in the best-of-nine) series with twelve hits, setting a World Series record that stood until 1964. He handled all thirty of his chances in the outfield without an error. Teammates testified that Jackson had not met with the gamblers; Claude "Lefty" Williams claimed that the players merely mentioned Jackson's name to the gamblers. Long forgotten beneath all those clouds of doubt is just how great a player Jackson was—so great that Babe Ruth said: "I copied his style because I thought he was the greatest hitter I'd ever seen. He's the guy who made me a hitter." Whatever Jackson's role was or wasn't in the scandal is now more than a century in the past. The time has come—put Shoeless Joe in the Hall of Fame.

A: Eddie Collins

What Are the Top 10 Most Revered Jersey Numbers (and Their Most Notable Bearers)?

Q: Who is the NFL's all-time leading touchdown scorer wearing number 32?

1. No. 32—Jim Brown, Magic Johnson, Sandy Koufax,
   O. J. Simpson
2. No. 8—Kobe Bryant, Alex Ovechkin, Cal Ripken Jr., Yogi Berra
3. No. 21—Roberto Clemente, Tim Duncan, Deion Sanders,
   LaDainian Tomlinson
4. No. 4—Bobby Orr, Lou Gehrig, Brett Favre, Jean Béliveau
5. No. 34—Walter Payton, Hakeem Olajuwon, Charles Barkley,
   David Ortiz
6. No. 7—John Elway, Mickey Mantle, Cristiano Ronaldo,
   Tina Thompson
7. No. 14—Pete Rose, Oscar Robertson, Ernie Banks, Bob Cousy
8. No. 20—Barry Sanders, Mike Schmidt, Frank Robinson, Ed Reed
9. No. 51—Dick Butkus, Randy Johnson, Ichiro Suzuki,
   Trevor Hoffman
10. No. 19—Johnny Unitas, Bob Feller, Tony Gwynn, Willis Reed

When we wrote *Got Your Number* a year ago, the most difficult decisions we had to make were on the selections for 4, 7, and 21. Choosing Bobby Orr over Lou Gehrig was excruciating. The selections of John Elway over Mickey Mantle and Roberto Clemente over both Deion Sanders and Tim Duncan generated the exact sort of passionate debate that book was intended for. Neither 32 nor 8 were nearly as challenging to choose among, which feels counterintuitive here, until you look closely at all the names on the list. Jim Brown, Magic Johnson, and Sandy Koufax all belong in the most exclusive wings of their respective halls of fame—I would argue they are the greatest running back, point guard, and big-game pitcher of all time. Had Kobe Bryant worn the number 8 his entire career I might have been inclined to flip the top two here, and if nothing else I used that to break what could easily be deemed a tie. (One further note: As of this writing, Ovechkin remains an active player. Should he surpass Wayne Gretzky's scoring record, once believed unbreakable, we reserve the right to revisit.)

 A: Marcus Allen (145)

What Are the Top 10 Legacy Positions in Major-Sports History?

Q: Who is the only Lakers center to win a scoring title since the team moved to Los Angeles in 1960?

1. Lakers Center
2. Packers Quarterback
3. Canadiens Goalie
4. Red Sox Left Fielder
5. Bears Linebacker
6. Dodgers Starting Pitcher
7. Bruins Defenseman
8. Yankees Center Fielder
9. Rams Defensive Lineman
10. Oilers Center

Wilt Chamberlain, Kareem Abdul-Jabbar, and Shaquille O'Neal are among the most dominant, and best remembered, players of their respective eras. But the lineage of the position did not start with any of them—it started well before, in the infancy of the sport, with a player who was equally dominant if not as well remembered. George Mikan joined the Minneapolis Lakers in 1947, two years before the formation of the NBA. That year, Mikan led the NBL (National Basketball League) in scoring, was named the league MVP, and led the Lakers to the championship. In all, Mikan would play seven seasons for the Lakers, averaging 23 points and over 13 rebounds per game. When he retired, he was the NBA's all-time leading scorer, and the Associated Press named him the greatest player of the first half of the century. While Mikan's achievements may not be widely remembered, the original big man remained well known by the giants of the game who followed in his footsteps. Shaq, in fact, paid for Mikan's funeral in 2005, explaining that "Without number 99, there is no me."

A: Shaquille O'Neal (29.7 PPG in 1999–2000)

Who Are the Top 12 QBs to Wear No. 12?

Q: Who was the opposing starting quarterback in Tom Brady's first NFL start?

1. Tom Brady	**7.** Ken Stabler
2. Aaron Rodgers	**8.** Bob Griese
3. Roger Staubach	**9.** Andrew Luck
4. Terry Bradshaw	**10.** John Brodie
5. Joe Namath	**11.** Rich Gannon
6. Jim Kelly	**12.** Randall Cunningham

The rivalry between Staubach and Bradshaw was probably not the greatest in the history of the sport. At minimum, Unitas vs. Starr, Marino vs. Elway, and Brady vs. Manning were all greater, in frequency at a minimum, and perhaps in magnitude as well. But I would argue that none of those was as *meaningful* to the growth of the NFL, and thus to the sport as a whole. Staubach and Bradshaw were the first quarterbacks ever to meet twice in the Super Bowl; Bradshaw's Steelers won both times, by a combined total of eight points. Still, to know only that is to understand almost nothing about what those games signified. The Steelers and Cowboys made America fall in love with pro football, transfixing and transforming a nation that has never strayed on any given Sunday since. And the faces of the respective franchises were the perfect illustrations of why. The clean-cut Naval officer, *Roger*, was the perfect leader for the buttoned-up, Hollywood-ready Cowboys, while the lovable country boy with the gap-toothed smile, *Terry*, led a hardworking, lunch-pail bunch that represented not only its own blue-collar city but seemingly all such cities at once. It is no coincidence that when the 1970s began, baseball was this nation's most popular sport, but by the end of the decade it no longer was.

 A: Peyton Manning (September 30, 2001)

What Are the Top 5 Craziest Things Actually Thrown on the Ice at a Professional Hockey Game?

Q: Which NHL franchise owns the record for most consecutive seasons making the playoffs?

1. Octopus (Red Wings)
2. Four-foot leopard shark (Sharks)
3. Hundreds of plastic rats (Panthers)
4. A live chicken (Kings)
5. Thousands of teddy bears (minor-league tradition)

The Legend of the Octopus is among the most fascinating sports traditions, one enjoyed, it seems, by many, but whose origin I fear is not well enough remembered. The tradition began in Detroit in 1952, a time when winning two best-of-seven series was required to win the Stanley Cup. Thus the eight arms of the octopus signified the eight wins necessary for the Red Wings to raise the cup. The practice began on April 15, when two brothers, Pete and Jerry Cusimano, whose family owned a fish store in the city's Eastern Market, hurled the first octopus into the rink at Olympia Stadium, where the Red Wings played from 1927–79. The team would sweep Toronto and Montreal to win the Stanley Cup, outscoring their playoff opponents 24–5. The brothers pronounced the octopus the reason the team won, and thus was a legend born.

A: **Boston Bruins | 29 straight seasons (1968–96)**

What Are the Top 10 Most Iconic Venues in Sports?

Q: Tiger Woods won the 2000 Open Championship at St Andrews at 19 under, breaking whose tournament score-to-par record?

1. St Andrews
2. Rose Bowl
3. Wrigley Field
4. Madison Square Garden
5. Augusta National
6. Lambeau Field

7. Churchill Downs
8. Indianapolis Motor Speedway
9. All England Lawn Tennis & Croquet Club
10. Rucker Park

So, here's the deal on St Andrews, aka The Old Course. It is not, in my opinion, anywhere near the best golf course in the world. It's not even the best course on this list, and within an hour's drive of the Swilcan Bridge you can play Kingsbarns, which I believe to be a far better and more enjoyable golf course as well. However, when it comes to history, nothing can touch it. We like to think of Wrigley Field and Fenway Park as historic because they date back to the early twentieth century. The Old Course is called the birthplace of golf because it is quite literally that: The game was first played on its links in the early fifteenth century. You would need far more space than we have here to begin to explain the impact St Andrews has had on the sport—but a key example of its import is that when the venue was first conceived, there were 22 holes, and the decision to combine several and thus create an 18-hole sport was made there in 1764. If you are ever so fortunate as to get the chance to visit, I have no doubt you will have your breath taken away by the history of the grounds, the cars parked ten yards off the 18th fairway, the Road Hole, and the Valley of Sin. In that moment it will not matter that you aren't on the best golf course in the world, because you will know you are in the place where it all began.

 A: Nick Faldo's (-18 in 1990)

What Are Greeny's Top 10 Golf Courses?

Q: Phil Mickelson is the winningest left-handed golfer in history (45 PGA Tour wins). Who ranks second?

1. Cypress Point
2. Royal County Down
3. Augusta National
4. Pine Valley
5. Sunningdale (Old)
6. Fishers Island
7. Royal Melbourne (West)
8. Royal Portrush
9. Royal Dornoch
10. Cabot Cliffs

There are very, very few things in life I love more than the game of golf. My family, my career, and . . . in all candor, that's probably about it. Golf is much more than a game; it is a spiritual pursuit. Every round is like a full lifetime, rife with drama, encompassing agony and ecstasy and, ultimately, acceptance. The game has taken me around the world, created memories that will last my lifetime, and nourished relationships that mean everything. I have enjoyed spending time on the golf course with people from all walks of life, of all sizes and shapes and backgrounds, and what I have invariably found is that I mostly like to play with people who only want to talk about golf while we're playing. Walking up a fairway is not the place to discuss the pennant race, or an NFL trade, or why your boss or your spouse are mad at you. The golf course is a place to detach from all of those; it provides a respite that, at least for me, nothing else can. I have said before and will say again: There is only one item on my bucket list and that is to someday shoot my age. I would love to do it in my sixties or seventies. If I have to wait until I reach my eighties, that's okay, too. On whatever the last day of my life is—and I hope it isn't for a long, long time—I hope on that day I spend time with my wife, my son, and my daughter, and I hope I play (at least) eighteen holes of golf.

 A: Bubba Watson (12)

16

What Are the Top 10 Most Memorable Modern Masters Moments?

Q: Jack Nicklaus won the 1986 Masters at the age of 46, breaking whose record for the oldest golfer to win the event?

1. "Yes, sir!" (1986, Jack Nicklaus)
2. "A win for the ages!" (1997, Tiger Woods)
3. "The return to glory!" (2019, Tiger Woods)
4. "In your life!" (2005, Tiger Woods)
5. Wedge from the woods (2012, Bubba Watson)
6. Blown six-shot lead (1996, Greg Norman)
7. Birdie from the bunker (1988, Sandy Lyle)
8. "Words do not do justice to the greatness of that shot." (1987, Larry Mize)
9. "Is it his time?" (2004, Phil Mickelson)
10. Spirit of Harvey Penick (1995, Ben Crenshaw)

In the modern history of The Masters, there have been endless thrills, too many to count, but it is easy to name the three most consequential tournaments, in chronological order: Nicklaus in 1986, Tiger in 1997, and then Tiger again in 2019. The two of them are inarguably the greatest players of the modern era. Woods is also the most significant, considering the game's dubious history with regard to race. Thus, I would posit that Tiger's first jacket, perfectly labeled "A win for the ages!" by Jim Nantz, is the most meaningful Masters victory in the history of the tournament. (As an aside: There has never, in my lifetime, been an announcer more perfectly suited for an event than Jim is at Augusta. If all of us were put on earth to do one thing, Jim Nantz's thing is to broadcast The Masters. But back to the matter at hand. . . .) Recency bias is a dangerous thing, because almost all of me wanted to put 2019 at the top of this list. Considering everything that had happened in Tiger's life, all the triumphs and all the despair, to see him win again, and this time to embrace his son, just as his own father had in the same exact spot twenty-two years before, it still gives me chills to imagine it. But, consider: Jack Nicklaus, the most accomplished player in the history of the sport, at age forty-six already six years removed from his most recent major championship, with just two PGA Tour wins in that span, shot 74 in the opening round, began the final day tied for ninth place, then shot 30 on the back nine to cap what was surely the most improbable, incredible, and memorable weekend in the storied history of the event. My favorite of all the brilliant descriptions written over the years came from columnist Thomas Boswell, who summed it up this way: "Some things cannot possibly happen, because they are both too improbable and too perfect. The U.S. hockey team cannot beat the Russians in the 1980 Olympics. Jack Nicklaus cannot shoot 65 to win The Masters at age 46. Nothing else comes immediately to mind."

 A: Gary Player (42 in 1978)

17

What Are the Top 10 Most Memorable Olympic Moments?

Q: Which school did Herb Brooks lead to three NCAA national championships in ice hockey (1974, 1976, 1979)?

1. Miracle on Ice (1980)
2. Jesse Owens wins four gold medals in Berlin (1936)
3. Tommie Smith and John Carlos civil rights protest (1968)
4. Muhammad Ali lights the Olympic Flame (1996)
5. Jim Redmond assists son, Derek, in finishing 400-meter race with torn hamstring (1992)
6. Nadia Comăneci scores first perfect 10 (1976)
7. Mary Lou Retton scores perfect 10s (1984)
8. North and South Korea march together (2000)
9. Kerri Strug clinches gold on injured ankle (1996)
10. Mutaz Essa Barshim and Gianmarco Tamberi share gold (2020)

If you are old enough, you will never forget those winter games at Lake Placid when we beat the Russians. Those were complicated times in America, and we desperately needed something we could all feel wonderful about. My most vivid recollection is of the Monday morning after the Miracle, after we'd gone on to beat Finland for the Gold Medal. In the locker room at school, someone started banging on a locker and cheering. "USA! USA!" Soon we were all doing it—banging on lockers and cheering as loudly as we could, a bunch of seventh graders, feeling pride in an American triumph. What makes the story unique is that I was a student at the United Nations International School. Only about half the kids in that room were American; the others were the children of diplomats from all over the world. But that didn't stop them from feeling proud. It was a victory for all of us. I don't think there's ever been anything quite like it in our country since, and sadly I'm not sure we will ever see anything like it again.

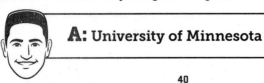
A: University of Minnesota

What Are the Top 7 Game 7 Performances?

Q: Which pitcher has the most career strikeouts across game sevens?

1. Jack Morris (1991 World Series)—10-inning shutout
2. Walt Frazier (1970 NBA Finals)—36 Pts, 19 Assts
3. Sandy Koufax (1965 World Series)—10-K shutout
4. LeBron James (2016 NBA Finals)—27-point triple-double, chase-down block
5. Kelly Hrudey (1987 Patrick Division Semifinals)—73 saves
6. Bill Russell (1962 NBA Finals)—53 Mins, 30 Pts, 40 Reb
7. Bill Mazeroski (1960 World Series)—walk-off HR

What Jack Morris did on the night of October 27, 1991, belongs on the wall of a museum, and not just the one in Cooperstown. It was a masterpiece every bit as much as *Mona Lisa* or *The Starry Night*. Further, if museums are places where history is remembered, then that performance, and what it represents, has been turned into a rare artifact by the modern game, a memory to be treasured because its like will never be seen again. The final pitching line for Morris that night reads: 10 innings, 7 hits, no runs, 2 walks, 8 strikeouts, and 122 pitches—the longest pitching performance ever in a seventh game of the World Series. (If you are a baseball fan under the age of thirty, I assure you that, yes, you are reading that correctly.) Moreover, Morris was making his third start of the series, each of the last two on short rest. And that game seven was made even more majestic, of course, because of the brilliance Morris was up against in John Smoltz and the Braves. It was a contest where the championship quite literally rode on every single pitch. It was the single best night to be a baseball fan of my entire life.

A: Bob Gibson (27, in 3 starts)

What Are the Top 10 Gutsiest Sports Performances?

Q: Who is the only player to outscore Michael Jordan head-to-head in an NBA playoff series?

1. Michael Jordan's "Flu Game" (1997 NBA Finals Game 5)
2. Kirk Gibson HR off Dennis Eckersley (1988 World Series Game 1)
3. Kerri Strug clinches gold on injured ankle (1996 Olympics)
4. Jack Youngblood plays with fractured fibula (1979 NFL playoffs)
5. Curt Schilling with bloody sock (2004 ALCS Game 6)
6. Brett Favre's 4 TDs the day after father dies (December 22, 2003)
7. Terell Owens has 9 Rec for 122 Yds 49 days after fracturing fibula and tearing ankle ligament (Super Bowl XXXIX)
8. Willis Reed plays with torn thigh muscle (1970 NBA Finals Game 7)
9. Isiah Thomas scores 43 points on sprained ankle (1988 NBA Finals Game 6)
10. Tiger Woods wins 2008 U.S. Open on one leg

*T*he Last Dance documentary covering Michael Jordan's career is one of my favorite programs that ESPN has created. And yet, Michael's story about the pizza he believes caused his digestive distress in Salt Lake City was one of the great disappointments of my sporting life. Not that it makes that much difference, I suppose, whether it was food poisoning or a stomach flu. Sick is sick, and his performance in any weakened condition speaks for itself: He scored 38 out of his team's 90 points to beat by 2 a Jazz squad that was 10–0 at home that postseason. However, "Flu Game" has become such a part of the vernacular of our culture—what golfer among us has not matched their career-best score while battling a nasty hangnail and proudly declared it their "flu game"?—that it feels deflating if its cause was not actually the flu.

A: Terry Cummings (1985 Eastern Conference First Round)

What Are the Top 10 Athlete Blunders?

Q: What was the starting pitching matchup in Game 6 of the 1986 World Series?

1. Bill Buckner
   (October 25, 1986)
2. Chris Webber (April 5, 1993)
3. Fred Brown (March 29, 1982)
4. Miracle at the Meadowlands
   (November 19, 1978)
5. Lindsey Jacobellis
   (February 17, 2006)
6. J. R. Smith (May 31, 2018)

7. Fred Merkle
   (September 23, 1908)
8. Leon Lett
   (November 25, 1993)
9. Jim Marshall
   (September 25, 1964)
10. Garo Yepremian
    (January 14, 1973)

The courage that it takes to play sports at the highest level is often overlooked (or perhaps consciously ignored). But the truth is that every player who reaches the peak of that mountain runs the risk of being eternally remembered for their worst moment. There is no greater illustration of this than Bill Buckner, who, tragically, is *only* remembered for the error he made behind the first-base bag in game six of the 1986 World Series, which cost the Red Sox a championship. What if I told you Buckner won a batting title, amassed 2,715 hits, and never struck out more than 39 times in any of his twenty-two seasons? Or that he set an MLB record for most assists by a first baseman in the same season that he led the National League in doubles? Buckner hit over .300 seven times, drove in 100 runs three times, and still holds the American League record for assists in a season. Ironically, he was an elite defensive first baseman, who was hobbled by leg injuries at the time he committed the career-defining error. Blessedly, he did not die with anger or spite in his heart. "Life is a lot of hard knocks," he said in 2016. "There are a lot worse things happening than losing a baseball game."

A: Roger Clemens (Red Sox) vs. Bob Ojeda (Mets)

What Are the Top 20 Team Nicknames in Sports History?

Q: Who is the only manager to win 10 American League pennants?

1. Murderers' Row (1927 Yankees)

2. Phi Slama Jama (1982–84 Houston men's basketball)

3. Fab Five (1991 Michigan men's basketball recruiting class)

4. Steel Curtain (1970s Steelers defensive line)

5. The Big Red Machine (1970s Reds)

6. Monsters of the Midway (Bears)

7. Bad Boys (1986–92 Pistons)

8. Dream Team (1992 United States men's Olympic basketball team)

9. Broad Street Bullies (1970s Flyers)

10. Bronx Bombers (Yankees)

11. America's Team (Cowboys)

12. Doomsday Defense (1960s–'70s Cowboys defense)

13. Greatest Show on Turf (1999–2001 Rams offense)

14. Fearsome Foursome (Deacon Jones, Merlin Olsen, Rosey Grier, Lamar Lundy)

15. The Pony Express (Eric Dickerson and Craig James)

16. The Boys of Summer (1950s Dodgers)

17. Splash Brothers (Stephen Curry and Klay Thompson)

18. Purple People Eaters (1968–77 Vikings defensive line)

19. Orange Crush (1970s–'80s Broncos defense)

20. New York Sack Exchange (Mark Gastineau, Joe Klecko, Marty Lyons, Abdul Salaam)

First of all—yes, we copped out. There was no way to limit this magnificent list to ten names, so we unilaterally made the decision to extend to twenty. Second—my *favorite* name on this list is Phi Slama Jama. It embodies everything that makes a nickname wonderful: It is amusing, accurate, and totally unique. The only thing it is not, however, is ubiquitous. Which is to say, it hasn't become a brand name. Nowhere in the culture do we refer to anything as "the Phi Slama Jama" of anything. Meanwhile, people to this day use the expression "Murderers' Row" all the time, and never in reference to Babe Ruth, Lou Gehrig, or Tony Lazzeri. The term was derived from the name applied to a section of the Tombs prison in New York City and was applied to various baseball teams before the Yankees made it forever their own. The 1927 Yankees, still the most legendary team in baseball history, featured six players who would make the Hall of Fame, as did the manager, Miller Huggins, and team president, Ed Barrow. Ruth led all baseball with 60 home runs that season, Gehrig was next with 47, and two players tied for third with 30 apiece. Gehrig led the way with 175 RBIs, Ruth was next with 164, and third place was at 131. I don't know that a week has gone by where I haven't referred to some team's upcoming schedule as a Murderers' Row. Larger than a nickname, it has become part of the vernacular and belongs at the top of this extraordinary list.

A: Casey Stengel

Who Are the Top 10 No. 1 Overall Picks in the Common Draft Era?

Q: Whose Cavaliers career scoring record did LeBron James break in 2008 at the age of 23?

1. LeBron James (NBA 2003)
2. Kareem Abdul-Jabbar (NBA 1969)
3. Mario Lemieux (NHL 1984)
4. Magic Johnson (NBA 1979)
5. Alex Ovechkin (NHL 2004)
6. Alex Rodriguez (MLB 1993)
7. Peyton Manning (NFL 1998)
8. Ken Griffey Jr. (MLB 1987)
9. John Elway (NFL 1983)
10. Guy Lafleur (NHL 1971)

You will not find a more accomplished list of historical greats anywhere you look, making this perhaps the most challenging group to rank. Strong arguments could be made for any of the top five names to ascend to number one. Ultimately, LeBron receives the edge for having surpassed Kareem as the NBA's all-time leading scorer. It has always been my contention that Abdul-Jabbar was the most accomplished basketball player that ever lived, but I can no longer defend that position; LeBron has earned his place atop the entire history of the sport. (To be perfectly clear: I still insist Michael Jordan is the *best* player that ever lived, which is an entirely different debate. Also, Jordan was not selected number one overall, so for the purposes of this list it doesn't make any difference.) Mario Lemieux deserves consideration for literally having saved the franchise for which he skated, twice. Had Super Mario not played for the Penguins, they would very likely have moved out of Pittsburgh. If he hadn't bought the team a generation later, they almost certainly would have. Finally, one further note: It was challenging to determine the proper place for Alex Rodriguez on this list, as his career statistics (696 home runs as an elite infielder) might warrant a much higher spot. We'll leave it to you to decide if we got it right.

 A: Brad Daugherty (10,389 points)

What Are the Top 10 Michael Jordan Single-Game NBA Performances?

Q: Michael Jordan is one of two players to score at least 60 points in a playoff game. Who is the other?

1. Playoff-record 63 points (April 20, 1986)
2. "The Shot" (May 7, 1989)
3. "Shrug Game" (June 3, 1992)
4. "Flu Game" (June 11, 1997)
5. Jordan over Russell (June 14, 1998)
6. "A Spectacular Move" (June 5, 1991)
7. 55 points in Finals Game 4 (June 16, 1993)
8. "Double-Nickel Game" (March 28, 1995)
9. 43 points at 40 years old (February 21, 2003)
10. Career-high 69 points (March 28, 1990)

When Michael Jordan set the postseason scoring record with 63 points, it caused Larry Bird to say, "I think it's just God disguised as Michael Jordan." Rather than repeat the endless reasons why that may have been the single greatest basketball game *anyone* ever played, let's instead focus on a night nine years later. March of 1995, Jordan had returned from the first of his premature retirements wearing number 45, and now it was his fifth game back and it still didn't quite feel real. The Bulls split his first four games, and Jordan looked rusty and, by his standards, tentative. The anticipation of his return to Madison Square Garden was extraordinary. I recall as I walked into the media entrance on 8th Avenue a fan shouted, "I'll give you five thousand dollars for your press pass!" Of course you know what happened that night—Jordan scored 55 (the double nickel) and won the game on a spectacular dish to Bill Wennington for an uncontested slam dunk. The sound in the arena told the entire story, growing as Jordan's night continued and his numbers climbed, reaching a deafening crescendo at the finish.

 A: Elgin Baylor (April 14, 1962)

Who Are the Top 10 Undrafted NFL Players in the Common Draft Era (Since 1967)?

Q: Which player caught the most touchdown passes thrown by Kurt Warner?

1. Kurt Warner
2. John Randle
3. Antonio Gates
4. Jason Peters
5. Warren Moon
6. Donnie Shell
7. Larry Little
8. Cliff Harris
9. Jeff Saturday
10. Drew Pearson

The life story of Kurt Warner is so improbable that if you had presented it as a Hollywood script you would have been laughed out of the room. Then he went ahead and lived it, and Hollywood made it into a movie. There aren't many more universally liked and admired players in football than Warner, in large part because of his kindness and decency. But I think there is more to it as well. I think Kurt epitomizes the dream all the players had at one time, a dream that got convoluted and confusing at whatever point the sport began to feel more like a business than a game. Because Kurt took the road less traveled and even less persevered, somewhere inside him the game remained a game throughout his career, through all the money, success, and fame. His appreciation for what he achieved was understandable and obvious to all, perhaps even contagious. Most NFL players have no idea what it actually feels like to stock shelves in a grocery store for $5.50 an hour. Kurt does. And the way he carries himself you can tell he has never forgotten. There have been many great underdog stories in football history, but there has never been anything like Kurt Warner. From the Hy-Vee grocery to the Hall of Fame, he is the personification of every unlikely dream that has ever come true.

A: Larry Fitzgerald (39, 48 including playoffs)

25

Who Are the Best QBs Selected in Each Round (1-17) of the NFL Draft?

Q: Bart Starr went 9–1 in his NFL playoff career. Which team beat him?

1. Patrick Mahomes (2017)

2. Brett Favre (1991)

3. Joe Montana (1979)

4. Sonny Jurgensen (1957)

5. Bob Waterfield (1944)

6. Tom Brady (2000)

7. Brock Purdy (2022)

8. Trent Green (1993)

9. Johnny Unitas (1955)

10. Roger Staubach (1964)

11. Doug Flutie (1985)

12. George Blanda (1949)

13. Charlie Conerly (1945)

14. Adrian Burk (1951)

15. Foster Watkins (1939)

16. Edd Hargett (1969)

17. Bart Starr (1956)

The first thing that jumped to mind as we concluded this list was: What kind of scouting was going on in the 1950s? I fully appreciate how different the sport, the position, and the world was. But, *come on*. Then, upon further inspection, I realized the cases of Unitas and Starr—the defining rivals and stars of their era—were both easy to understand. Unitas attended Louisville, hardly a football powerhouse, and he suffered so many injuries his senior season he actually finished second on his team in passing. As for Starr, while he played at Alabama, he hardly played at all in either of his final two seasons because of a back injury he suffered during fraternity initiation. The two would, of course, go on to carry professional football into the modern era. They would combine to win eight championships and four MVP awards. Had there been Twitter, or even sports talk radio, in the 1960s, the number one driving topic would have been *Who is better, Starr or Unitas?* For the purposes of this list, no such decision must be made. For once, these two giants of the game equally belong.

A: Eagles (1960 NFL Championship)

26

What Are the Top Months in the Sports Calendar?

Q: Who joined Reggie "Mr. October." Jackson (1973 Athletics, 1977 Yankees) as the only other position player to win multiple World Series MVPs?

1. October

2. April

3. November

4. September

5. March

6. December

7. January

8. June

9. May

10. February

11. August

12. July

Let's start with full disclosure: While I am as passionate a sports fan as you have ever known, and try as hard as I can to represent as such on all my shows, I am also a veteran of more than thirty years in the sports broadcasting business and there is absolutely no way for me to divorce my professional bias from this question. Thus, while The Masters is my single favorite sporting event, and while the start of baseball means the coming of spring, I cannot choose April over October, simply because it doesn't have football in it. Football is the ultimate difference maker in my business; I have been known to say "I work seven months a year; the other five are football season." Thus does October edge April, and for the exact same reason does July find itself at the back of the line. The week of the MLB All-Star Game, which hasn't had near the luster it once did anyhow, contains the only days of the entire sporting calendar completely void of sports activity. This is why you have a better chance of seeing your favorite sports talk show hosts on a golf course in July than you do on television.

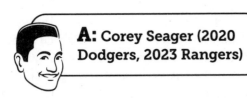

A: Corey Seager (2020 Dodgers, 2023 Rangers)

What Are the Top 10 Days on the Annual Sporting Calendar?

Q: What is the name of the song that has been played at the end of every NCAA Tournament since 1987?

1. Opening Thursday of March Madness
2. Super Bowl Sunday
3. NFL Draft
4. Masters Sunday
5. MLB Opening Day
6. Thanksgiving Saturday
7. NFL Thanksgiving Day
8. NFL Conference Championship Sunday
9. Kentucky Derby Saturday
10. NBA Christmas Day

I have said it many times and it continues to be true: If you allowed me only one day of televised sports in the calendar year, I would choose Sunday at The Masters. Thus, it pained me to place Augusta at number four on this list. But the truth is, while I look forward to that day every year, it does not always deliver. The three above it on this list *always* do. There is nothing quite like the first day of the NCAA Tournament; it is no coincidence that urologists across the country have reported increases of as much as 50 percent in the number of vasectomies scheduled in the days leading up to it. What better way to spend a day or two sitting on the couch with a bag of ice on your lap than watching fourteen hours of basketball? Two factors make it the best day of the year. First, the sheer length of the experience: From noon until well past midnight, there is never a moment when there isn't at least one game to watch. Second, the day is genuinely too big to fail: When you have sixteen games to watch, it is next to impossible for none of them to be memorable. Upsets, Cinderellas, buzzer beaters, bands playing, cheerleaders crying, iconic theme music, and every man, woman, and child alive holding at least one bracket in their hands; there is simply nothing in the world better than the onset of the Madness of March.

 A: "One Shining Moment"

28

Who Are the Top 10 Heavyweight Boxers of All Time?

Q: Which heavyweight recorded the second-most consecutive title defenses after Joe Louis's 25?

1. Muhammad Ali
2. Joe Louis
3. Rocky Marciano
4. George Foreman
5. Joe Frazier
6. Larry Holmes
7. Jack Dempsey
8. Jack Johnson
9. Lennox Lewis
10. Evander Holyfield

Perhaps the most interesting thing about this list is a name that isn't on it. The place that Mike Tyson occupied in our culture, well beyond the limited realm of sports, was as significant as that of practically any other athlete of his era. The trouble is, if you blinked, you missed it. Hard as it is to believe for those of us who remember so vividly his star power and utter dominance in the ring, Tyson only defended his title of lineal heavyweight champion twice before he was stunningly knocked out by Buster Douglas in Japan. In fact, the span of time between Tyson's apex in the ring—his first-round knockout of Michael Spinks, in what was then the richest fight in boxing history—and his loss to Douglas was a mere eighteen months. Tyson engendered as much fear, and built as much fame, as any fighter on this list, but ultimately his accomplishments as a boxer simply did not measure up to those mentioned above.

A: Larry Holmes (20)

29

What Are the Top 10 Muhammad Ali Quotes?

Q: Who are the only two boxers Muhammad Ali fought three times in his professional career?

1. "I am the greatest, I said that even before I knew I was."
2. "Float like a butterfly. Sting like a bee. You can't hit what your eyes don't see."
3. "I shook up the world. Me! Whee!"
4. "A man who views the world the same at fifty as he did at twenty has wasted thirty years of his life."
5. "It isn't the mountains ahead that wear you down. It's the pebble in your shoe."
6. "*Impossible* is just a word thrown around by small men who find it easier to live in the world they've been given than to explore the power they have to change it. Impossible is not a fact. It's an opinion. Impossible is potential. Impossible is temporary. Impossible is nothing."
7. "If you even dream of beating me you'd better wake up and apologize."
8. "A man who has no imagination has no wings."
9. "I've wrestled with alligators. I've tussled with a whale. I done handcuffed lightning. And thrown thunder in jail."
10. "Service to others is the rent you pay for your room here on earth."

I chose the first quote here because I believe it is so deeply meaningful. Something far more than witty, I see it as clear evidence of just how far ahead of his time Ali was. Decades before "speaking it into existence" was a phrase anyone thought to use, Ali was manifesting his destiny.

 A: Joe Frazier and Ken Norton

30

What Are the Top 10 Rivalries in Tennis History?

Q: Either Chris Evert or Martina Navratilova finished every year ranked number one from 1975–86. Who broke that streak in 1987?

1. Martina Navratilova–Chris Evert
2. Roger Federer–Rafael Nadal–Novak Djokovic
3. Serena Williams–Venus Williams
4. John McEnroe–Björn Borg
5. Rod Laver–Ken Rosewall
6. Pete Sampras–Andre Agassi
7. Steffi Graf–Monica Seles
8. John McEnroe–Jimmy Connors
9. Margaret Court–Billie Jean King
10. Stefan Edberg–Ivan Lendl

Nothing and no one will ever compare to Chrissie and Martina. Theirs was the greatest rivalry in the modern history of sports—greater than Magic and Bird, Ali and Frazier, or anyone else. We made that an open-and-shut case in *Got Your Number*, using this insane statistic (among many others): Evert and Navratilova met in the finals of sixty tournaments. *Sixty!* By comparison, Federer and Nadal met in 24 finals, Federer and Djokovic 19, and Nadal and Djokovic 29. In fact, let's go one step deeper. Federer vs. Nadal at one time appeared to be shaping up as the greatest rivalry in the history of the men's game. Consider, then, that in their entire careers they met a total of forty times. Chrissie and Martina played in sixty *finals*! The number truly boggles the mind. When you further consider the implications of the times, their contrast in styles, and the growth of the women's game in general in the 1970s, there is only one conclusion to be reached. Chris Evert and Martina Navratilova created a rivalry in their careers that has never been matched and seems unlikely to be approached anytime soon.

A: Steffi Graf

31

What Are the Top 5 Rivalries in College Football History?

Q: Roger Staubach is one of two players in the Pro Football Hall of Fame who attended Army/Navy. Who is the other?

1. Army–Navy
2. Michigan–Ohio State
3. Alabama–Auburn (Iron Bowl)
4. Oklahoma–Texas (Red River Showdown)
5. Harvard–Yale (The Game)

The first time Army faced Navy on the football field was November 29, 1890. In the more than thirteen decades that have passed since, almost no event in our nation has remained as meaningful, nor as true to its original ethos. The annual game itself is so much more than the ten sitting US presidents who have attended, or the star players—such as Roger Staubach and Doc Blanchard—who have competed in it. Bigger even than the fact this game featured the first time a helmet was worn during a football game (1893) and the inaugural use of instant replay in any sport (1963). This game is our best illustration that rivalry can be respectful, that opponents need not be enemies, that victory need not come at the expense of dignity. In other words, it is about lessons that applied back in the 1800s and still apply today—perhaps more than ever—well beyond the fields of play. For as long as the game has been played and as long as it continues, Army vs. Navy is a reminder that what is always most important about the best games in sports history is not who won and who lost, but simply that they were played at all.

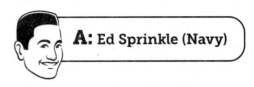

A: Ed Sprinkle (Navy)

32

Who Are the Top 10 College Football Players to Never Win the Heisman (Awarded Since 1935)?

Q: Jim Brown is one of three Syracuse running backs in the Pro Football Hall of Fame. Who are the other two?

1. Jim Brown (Syracuse)
2. Peyton Manning (Tennessee)
3. Dick Butkus (Illinois)
4. Gale Sayers (Kansas)
5. Deion Sanders (Florida State)
6. Adrian Peterson (Oklahoma)
7. Chuck Bednarik (Penn)
8. Marshall Faulk (San Diego State)
9. Bubba Smith (Michigan State)
10. Reggie White (Tennessee)

If you forced me to choose the single best player to ever set foot on a gridiron, it would be Jim Brown. Had he not cut his own NFL career short, I believe there would be common consensus around that. His greatness was on display only in glimpses, however, during his collegiate career. As a freshman in 1953, Brown was the only African American player on the Syracuse team and endured all manner of racist indignities, including the coaches trying to move him to a different position. In his second year, Brown was the team's second leading rusher. As a junior, Brown rushed for over 600 yards, but it was not until his final season, 1956, that he was a first-team All-American. Brown rushed for 986 yards that season despite Syracuse playing only eight games. He finished fifth in the Heisman voting, well behind the winner, Paul Hornung, as well as Johnny Majors, Tommy McDonald, and Jerry Tubbs. The vote is considered one of the most controversial in the history of the award—Hornung played for a losing team and it was widely accepted that Brown was the best player—but many of the voters refused to consider Black candidates. Hornung was subsequently drafted number one overall by the Packers; Brown went number six to Cleveland, one spot behind Hall of Fame QB Len Dawson.

 A: Floyd Little and Larry Csonka

33

Who Are the Top 10 Players in the History of the Negro Leagues?

Q: Who was the first Hall of Fame electee of the Committee on Negro Baseball Leagues?

1. Josh Gibson
2. Oscar Charleston
3. Satchel Paige
4. Bullet Rogan
5. Buck Leonard
6. John Henry "Pop" Lloyd
7. Turkey Stearnes
8. Cool Papa Bell
9. Willie Wells
10. Smokey Joe Williams

Babe Ruth was the white Josh Gibson. People who really know baseball history know that to be the case despite the fact that the comparison is more commonly used in reverse. Yes, Ruth was the most important star in the sport, raising the spotlight it enjoyed to levels that previously would have seemed unimaginable. And, yes, he was a tremendous ballplayer. He just wasn't the greatest that ever lived. Gibson was that—and the records now finally show it. In 2020, MLB announced it would recognize Negro League statistics, including the .465 Gibson hit in 1943, the second-highest single-season batting average ever. Historians believe Gibson hit approximately 800 home runs, with a listed career batting average of .373 for his seventeen-season career. He won the Triple Crown in 1936 and 1937 and remains the last player ever to do so in consecutive seasons. Gibson died at the age of 35, just months before Jackie Robinson played his first game for the Dodgers. Years later, Larry Doby, the first Black player in the American League, said, "One of the things that was disappointing and disheartening to a lot of the Black players at the time was that Jack was not the best player. The best was Josh Gibson. I think that's one of the reasons why Josh died so early—he was heartbroken."

A: Satchel Paige (1971)

What Is the Perfect All-Time Baseball Lineup, According to Hembo?

Q: Which AL/NL player has come closest to batting .400 since Ted Williams did so in 1941?

1. Barry Bonds (LF)
2. Babe Ruth (RF)
3. Josh Gibson (C)
4. Ted Williams (DH)
5. Rogers Hornsby (2B)
6. Lou Gehrig (1B)
7. Willie Mays (CF)
8. Mike Schmidt (3B)
9. Honus Wagner (SS)
• Walter Johnson (SP)

Behold—the most perfect lineup ever constructed to maximize run-scoring output. You might find Babe Ruth a peculiar choice for the two-hole, but hear me out: For a century and a half, managers would position their best hitter third or fourth in the order to provide more RBI opportunities. Analytics have debunked that logic. The ideal position for your best hitter is the two-hole, which provides the ideal blend of RBI opportunities *and* plate appearances. Over 162 games, Ruth will come to the plate 30–40 more times batting second than he would batting, say, cleanup. This philosophy is now pervasive in the modern game—in 2022, Aaron Judge—a 6' 7" slugger—hit 47 of his 62 home runs from the two-hole. Analytics are here to stay—either get in line or get out of the way.

A: Tony Gwynn (.394 in 1994)

35

What Is the Perfect All-Time Baseball Lineup, According to Greeny?

Q: What is the only franchise for which three players hit 500 home runs?

1. Rickey Henderson (LF)
2. Joe DiMaggio (CF)
3. Hank Aaron (RF)
4. Babe Ruth (DH)
5. Lou Gehrig (1B)

6. Alex Rodriguez (SS)
7. Johnny Bench (C)
8. Brooks Robinson (3B)
9. Pete Rose (2B)
• Sandy Koufax (SP)

Hembo's lineup is the perfect illustration of all that is wrong with decisions being purely driven by analytics. What he put together is a list of the best players at every position. What it is *not* is a team. The simple truth is, Rickey Henderson is not only the greatest leadoff hitter that ever lived, he is the living embodiment of what the role was meant to be. Barry Bonds may ultimately have risen to greater heights, but if the game is still the game, the objective of the first batter is to get on base and then make things happen. You can have Bonds swinging for the fences all you want; Henderson will still wind up scoring more runs. Analytics, Hembo, get this one wrong.

 A: Giants (Willie Mays, 646; Barry Bonds, 586; Mel Ott, 511)

36

What Are the Top 10 World Series Performances by a Position Player?

Q: Who is the only player to homer in four consecutive games to end a single World Series?

1. 1977 Reggie Jackson
2. 2011 David Freese
3. 1928 Lou Gehrig
4. 1972 Gene Tenace
5. 2013 David Ortiz
6. 1956 Yogi Berra
7. 1970 Brooks Robinson
8. 1971 Roberto Clemente
9. 1967 Lou Brock
10. 2002 Barry Bonds

It was October 18, 1977, and Yankee Stadium was the loudest place on planet Earth. Reggie Jackson, baseball's most magnetic and polarizing star, was walking toward home plate with a bat in his hand. Under any circumstances, that was a moment to cherish. But in the eighth inning that night, game six of the World Series, the crowd rose to its feet as one, creating a deafening roar as the legendary announcer Keith Jackson set the stage on ABC. "Reggie Jackson has seen two pitches in the strike zone tonight, and he's hit them both in the seats." A few seconds later, the first pitch from Charlie Hough became the third, and even Howard Cosell could not be heard above the din. The home run was not only Jackson's third of the night, it was his fifth in three games, driving in eight runs—he finished that series with a record 25 total bases. Thus was born the legend of "Mister October," which has to rank high on the all-time list of greatest sports nicknames. There are other performances on this list whose numbers would suggest they surpass what Reggie did that year, but this is where numbers fail to tell the full story. That night at Yankee Stadium was about much more than numbers, much more than home runs. It was about how baseball can somehow matter more than anything in the world when it all comes together just right. And that night, it was just right.

 A: George Springer (2017 Astros)

37

Who Has Baseball's Top 10 Prettiest Swings?

Q: Who was the only player to hit more home runs during the 1990s than Ken Griffey Jr.'s 382?

1. Ken Griffey Jr.
2. Ted Williams
3. Joe DiMaggio
4. Shoeless Joe Jackson
5. Rod Carew

6. Chipper Jones
7. Miguel Cabrera
8. Darryl Strawberry
9. Ichiro Suzuki
10. Steve Garvey

Ken Griffey Jr. left the game of baseball with any number of claims to fame, including being the first ever number one overall pick to make it to the Hall of Fame. Further, the image of his huge grin, cap on backwards, while he launched batting practice blast after blast, remains about the most fun visual the sport has ever produced. But, when the story of Griffey's career is written, none of those are in the opening paragraph. The first words that spring from the pens, or mouths, of anyone who ever watched him are always: "Well, he had that swing. . . ." Indeed, he did. A swing so pretty we were all better for having seen it. A swing that looked like it came with the instructional video for the game itself. A swing so perfect it actually defied description. As a golfer, it reminds me of watching Fred Couples swing a golf club: so balanced, so perfect, so impossibly coordinated, so effortless and yet so powerful. While we await new and better adjectives getting added to the English language for the sake of describing this swing, I'll just turn the commentary over to a few folks you know. "His grace and power were unmatched."—Johnny Bench. "He had the prettiest swing I have ever seen."—Barry Larkin. "His swing is perfect, I said it and I still believe it."—Bobby Valentine.

A: Mark McGwire (405)

38

What Are the Top 10 Best Pitches in Baseball History?

Q: What pitcher's record for consecutive scoreless innings in the postseason did Mariano Rivera break in 2000?

1. Mariano Rivera's cutter
2. Walter Johnson's fastball
3. Sandy Koufax's curveball
4. Nolan Ryan's fastball
5. Christy Mathewson's fadeaway
6. Randy Johnson's slider
7. Phil Niekro's knuckleball
8. Satchel Paige's hesitation
9. Fernando Valenzuela's screwball
10. Pedro Martínez's changeup

"**Y**ou know what's coming," an opposing hitter once said, of facing Mariano Rivera, "but you know what's coming in horror movies, too." Beyond all of the amazing statistics Rivera achieved, the most amazing part is that he amassed them all without hardly ever attempting to fool a hitter. Pitcher vs. hitter is baseball's game of chess, but for Rivera it was as though every one of his pieces was a queen. No strategy—not the French defense, the London System, or the Queen's Gambit—is going to beat that. That's how Rivera became the king of the mound, aka "the best at his position by a wider margin than any player at any position in the history of baseball" according to columnist Tom Verducci. His one pitch, the cutter, left his hand looking exactly the same as his fastball, rendering it practically unhittable. I would posit that Rivera's cutter and Kareem Abdul-Jabbar's skyhook are the two most unassailable munitions ever carried in the arsenal of sports. The shot led Kareem to the top of the NBA's all-time scoring list, while the pitch led Rivera to becoming the first unanimous choice to the Hall of Fame baseball ever had.

A: Whitey Ford's (33 ⅔ in 1960–62)

39

What Are the Top 10 Signature Moves in Basketball History?

Q: Who is the only UCLA player to average 25 points in a season since Kareem Abdul-Jabbar (then known as Lew Alcindor)?

1. Kareem Abdul-Jabbar's skyhook
2. Michael Jordan's fadeaway
3. George Gervin's finger roll
4. Allen Iverson's crossover
5. Hakeem Olajuwon's dream shake
6. Stephen Curry's pull-up three
7. LeBron James's chase-down block
8. Magic Johnson's no-look pass
9. Dirk Nowitzki's one-legged fadeaway
10. Tim Duncan's bank shot

To fully appreciate the perfection of the skyhook, you have to *really* watch it. There is something so elegant, majestic, and coordinated about the act, it makes the un-flashiest possible play on a basketball court look cool. (The other such play, the underhand free throw—or so-called "granny" shot—as perfected by Rick Barry, was also endlessly effective, but never looked the slightest bit cool and nobody tried to imitate it.) Kareem himself said: "It's not a hard shot to learn," and yet no one since him has ever seemed willing or able to learn it. Perhaps some analytics geek (no offense, Hembo) should examine the efficiency and begin forcing it on their players. Kareem recorded the first three 30 PPG seasons on 55 percent shooting, and did so consecutively from 1971–73. Over the course of his twenty seasons, he shot 56 percent from the floor, and 53 percent in 237 career playoff games. There are plenty of reasons Kareem is among the most accomplished players in the history of basketball, but the skyhook is number one on the list.

 A: Reggie Miller (25.9 PPG in 1986)

40

Who Are the Top 10 Shooters in NBA History?

Q: Which team had the fifth and sixth picks in the 2009 NBA Draft, passing on Stephen Curry with both and allowing the Warriors to draft Curry with seventh pick?

1. Stephen Curry
2. Larry Bird
3. Reggie Miller
4. Chris Mullin
5. Kevin Durant

6. Ray Allen
7. Steve Kerr
8. Klay Thompson
9. Mark Price
10. J. J. Redick

Let's face it, the top of this list required no thought at all. Ranking two through ten was a stressful exercise. But number one? A walk in the park. Steph Curry has completely revolutionized the sport, changed it forever in ways that only a small handful of players ever did before. As a weapon, he has the equal but opposite reaction on defenses as Shaquille O'Neal had. Both were unstoppable, but whereas Shaq collapsed defenses until they imploded, Curry stretches them until they snap like an elastic band. And he does it with such panache. Not only does he have unprecedented range, he also shoots it off the dribble more effectively than any player who ever lived. Our colleague Stephen A. Smith has it right, and puts it perhaps most simply, when he calls Steph "the best shooter God ever created." He gets no argument out of me, nor from literally anyone else.

A: Timberwolves (drafted Ricky Rubio and Jonny Flynn)

41

Who Are the Top 10 Passers in NBA History?

Q: Whose record for career playoff assists did Magic Johnson break in 1985?

1. Magic Johnson
2. Larry Bird
3. Jason Kidd
4. LeBron James
5. John Stockton

6. Oscar Robertson
7. Steve Nash
8. Chris Paul
9. Nikola Jokić
10. Bob Cousy

Earvin Johnson didn't get his nickname because of the numbers he put up; he is called "Magic" because he was among the most dynamic, compelling, bewilderingly brilliant people ever to handle a basketball. It almost feels like doing him a disservice to write up all the assist numbers he posted; to truly appreciate Magic Johnson you have to have seen him play. Still, more than ever before, players are measured by their measurables, so here they come. Johnson led the NBA in assists in four different seasons and remains the career leader in assists per game. In the biggest games, he was even better: Johnson is the NBA's all-time leader in postseason assists, and his 12.3 per game is the highest rate in playoff history as well. So, the credentials are intact. But, if those are all you know, you have no idea why he was known as Magic. The joy with which he played, the creativity with which he ran the fast break, the vision and savvy touch he displayed on seemingly every possession of his career were the truly profound things about him. Magic Johnson was not merely the best passer the game ever saw, he was also by far the most fun to watch.

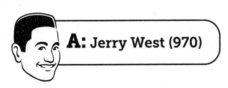

A: Jerry West (970)

42

Who Are the Top 10 Defenders in NBA History?

Q: Who is the only player to average fewer points in an MVP season than Bill Russell's 14.1 in 1964–65?

1. Bill Russell
2. Hakeem Olajuwon
3. Tim Duncan
4. Dikembe Mutombo
5. Michael Jordan
6. Gary Payton
7. Dennis Rodman
8. Kevin Garnett
9. Scottie Pippen
10. Walt Frazier

This one isn't close. Bill Russell is to the NBA what Bobby Orr, Lawrence Taylor, and Ozzie Smith are to their respective sports: the greatest defensive player ever. His prowess in rebounding and shot blocking were the stuff of legend, stemming from his extraordinary jumping ability; during his collegiate track and field career, Russell was ranked the seventh best high jumper in the world. That ability enabled Russell to become the most feared shot blocker in NBA history—his blocks were known as "Wilsonburgers," referring to the Wilson basketballs he shoved back into the faces of opposing shooters. Statistics on blocked shots were not kept in the NBA until well after Russell's career, but it has been credibly estimated that he blocked eight shots per game; the official NBA record is held by Mark Eaton at 3.5 per game. Russell was also the greatest rebounder to ever play, averaging 22.5 rebounds per game for his career, and an almost unthinkable 25 per game in the playoffs. When they say "defense wins championships," Bill Russell is what they are talking about, the man whose defense made his Celtics the greatest dynasty in the history of American professional sports.

A: Wes Unseld (13.8 PPG in 1968–69)

43

Who Are the Top 10 In-Game Dunkers in NBA History?

Q: Julius Erving is one of two players to win multiple MVPs in the ABA (1974, 1975, 1976). Who is the other?

1. Julius Erving
2. Michael Jordan
3. Vince Carter
4. Blake Griffin
5. Kobe Bryant
6. Dominique Wilkins
7. Shawn Kemp
8. LeBron James
9. David Thompson
10. Darryl Dawkins

A few caveats are necessary here. The first is that dunking in games is vastly different from a dunk contest; if we were judging the greatest dunk contest performances, Vince Carter would be number one by a wide margin. He merited a place on this list as well because of the ferocity of his slams and the way he took it to defenders; it is safe to say no one put more NBA players on posters than Carter did. The second is to acknowledge that no one ever took your breath away dunking in games the way Michael Jordan did—when he got out ahead on a break you could hear the anticipation in the building coming through your television. So, Michael could easily have been number one here. But I went with Doctor J because I feel like had he not come first there may have been no Michael. The way the game is played now—above the rim—is certainly not the way it always was. Erving was not the game's first great dunker, but he *was* the one who turned the dunk into an art form. Said otherwise: He put the slam in the slam dunk. As Hembo and I went back and forth on this one, I found myself thinking, "Michael himself would want us to put Erving on top, because *he* paved the way." That settled it.

 A: Mel Daniels (1969, 1971)

44

Who Are the Top 10 Duos in NBA History?

Q: In 1993–94, playing without Michael Jordan, Scottie Pippen finished third in MVP voting behind which players?

1. Michael Jordan and Scottie Pippen
2. Kareem Abdul-Jabbar and Magic Johnson
3. Shaquille O'Neal and Kobe Bryant
4. Bill Russell and Bob Cousy
5. Kevin Durant and Stephen Curry
6. LeBron James and Dwyane Wade
7. Moses Malone and Julius Erving
8. Jerry West and Wilt Chamberlain
9. Karl Malone and John Stockton
10. Stephen Curry and Klay Thompson

The unseemly disintegration of the relationship between Michael Jordan and Scottie Pippen has brought genuine sadness to many, me among them, because of all the joy and magic they brought into our lives. Theirs was always a complicated relationship. As a reporter who was around their teams for years, I heard Scottie asked countless times what it was like to play with Michael, and never once did he waver in his admiration. Far less frequently was Jordan asked about Pippen, but I can attest that he never once failed to offer enormous credit to his teammate for all they accomplished. However, there could never be true balance in their dynamic: Jordan was the greatest player ever, and Pippen was his brilliant sidekick—a Hall of Famer himself, but a sidekick nonetheless. It cannot have been easy for Scottie, and I think what we see today is mostly a byproduct of that. (The relationship between Jordan's son and Pippen's ex-wife is not, nor should it be, overlooked here, but I stand by my belief that the issues predated and will outlast that situation.) Sad it all is, because the two of them were the perfect basketball pairing and created a decade of excitement seldom equaled in the history of sports. Combining for six championships puts them on the same level with Russell and Cousy, one ahead of Kareem and Magic, with a better winning percentage together than either of those pairings. For my money, Shaq and Kobe were actually the most dominant duo, but that was only for a short time; their accomplishments simply do not stand up alongside their predecessors from Chicago.

 A: Hakeem Olajuwon and David Robinson

Who Are the Top 10 NFL Coach-QB Duos of All Time?

Q: What was the only team to have a winning record against the Belichick–Brady Patriots (including playoffs)?

1. Bill Belichick–Tom Brady (Patriots)
2. Bill Walsh–Joe Montana (49ers)
3. Andy Reid–Patrick Mahomes (Chiefs)
4. Vince Lombardi–Bart Starr (Packers)
5. Chuck Noll–Terry Bradshaw (Steelers)
6. Tom Landry–Roger Staubach (Cowboys)
7. Mike Holmgren–Brett Favre (Packers)
8. Sean Payton–Drew Brees (Saints)
9. Paul Brown–Otto Graham (Browns)
10. Marv Levy–Jim Kelly (Bills)

This is a category to which I devoted a great deal of thought. The easiest measurement here would simply be *actual* measurement: *How many rings did each duo win?* Important. But I believe there is much more than that at play. To me, championships are the table stakes in a category such as this, while the *real* differentiation comes in more esoteric categories, such as stature, innovation, dominance, and lasting impact. By either metric, Belichick and Brady are an easy choice at number one; they ace all the criteria above, while also hoarding the most jewelry. However, while many will quibble with my selection of Walsh/Montana ahead of the more decorated pairings that follow them, I believe those Niners teams belong because they revolutionized the sport. Prior to their artistic offensive explosion, the adage "defense wins championships" was the law of the NFL. And, not coincidentally, it has never really been true in their wake. After the West Coast offense took hold—and others were able to see what had previously existed only in Walsh's imagination—the game was never the same.

A: Broncos (9–8 vs. the Pats)

What Are the Top 5 Father-Son Sports Moments?

Q: Tiger Woods led the PGA Tour in wins in every season from 1999–2009, save for 2004. Which golfer led that season?

1. Tiger Woods celebrates first major (1997) with father, Earl, and fifteenth major (2019) with son, Charlie

2. Michael Jordan clinches fourth title on Father's Day, 1996 (first title after father, James, was murdered in 1993)

3. Ken Griffey and Ken Griffey Jr. hit back-to-back home runs (September 14, 1990)

4. Jim Redmond assists son, Derek, in finishing 400-meter race at 1992 Olympics (torn hamstring)

5. Jack Harbaugh watches his sons, John and Jim, coach Super Bowl XLVII

The image of a man and his son embracing on the 18th green of the most celebrated golf course in the world came full circle in 2019. Tiger Woods, the most dynamic athlete his sport has ever seen, was in on both hugs, first as the son, and then as the father. When he embraced Earl Woods in 1997, after the "win for the ages," it was the end of the beginning. For years, Earl had brashly predicted that Tiger would someday change the world, and in that moment he had. It's hard to quantify all the water that went under the Hogan Bridge between that day and the one that came 22 years later. That day, Earl was present in spirit only, while it felt as though Tiger had lived a dozen lifetimes in the intervening years. Through it all, what was never lost was the world's fascination with everything Tiger did. And so when he won again, against all odds, and then lifted his own son in his arms, it was both the same and entirely different. And it was somehow better than it had ever been before.

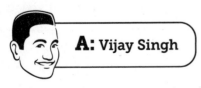

A: Vijay Singh

47

Who Are the Top 10 Athlete Siblings?

Q: Serena Williams beat her sister, Venus, 19 times head-to-head. Who is the only player she beat more times?

1. Venus & Serena Williams

2. Jason & Travis Kelce

3. Mack & Jackie Robinson

4. Peyton & Eli Manning

5. Cheryl & Reggie Miller

6. Phil & Tony Esposito

7. Vitali & Wladimir Klitschko

8. Sterling & Shannon Sharpe

9. Maurice & Henri Richard

10. Clay & Bruce Matthews

Despite the countless millions of words written and hours put onto screens devoted to the story of Venus and Serena Williams, I often wonder if the astonishing magnitude of their success has ever been fully appreciated. Consider: These granddaughters of Louisiana sharecroppers were raised in Compton, California, a city with the highest crime rate in the state at that time. By the time Venus, the older of the two, was twenty-three, the sisters were ranked 1 and 2 in the world in singles, a distinction they would hold again eight years later. Between them they would win 30 Grand Slam singles titles, 28 Grand Slam doubles titles, 4 Grand Slam mixed doubles titles, and 8 Olympic Gold Medals. Perhaps the best summary of their shared life experience came from Venus, on *The Oprah Winfrey Show* in 2002: "It's definitely a strange situation to be in because no one else has been in this position Serena and I are in," she said. "But all in all the best part is that right now we are the best at what we do."

 A: Maria Sharapova (20)

48

Who Are the Top 10 Individual Winter Olympians?

Q: What is the only US city to host multiple Winter Olympics?

1. Bjørn Dæhlie (Norwegian cross-country skier)
2. Sonja Henie (Norwegian figure skater)
3. Ole Einar Bjørndalen (Norwegian biathlete)
4. Marit Bjørgen (Norwegian cross-country skier)
5. Ireen Wüst (Dutch speed skater)
6. Kjetil André Aamodt (Norwegian alpine skier)
7. Eric Heiden (American speed skater)
8. Matti Nykänen (Finnish ski jumper)
9. Shaun White (American snowboarder)
10. Katarina Witt (German figure skater)

Not only have you likely not heard Dæhlie's name since his last Olympics in 1998, you likely couldn't get your keyboard to spell it properly if I gave you an hour. That said, the man is a national hero in his native Norway and the most decorated Winter Olympian of all time. Racing in three different Olympics, Dæhlie won 12 medals, 8 of them gold, and would almost certainly have added to his total in 2002 had a freak roller-skiing accident (yes, you read that correctly) not left him with back injuries so severe he was never again able to compete, no matter his extensive attempts at rehabilitation. His retirement stunned his home nation, where he remains a beloved figure to this day. A final note, solely because I find it fascinating: During the winter season, the average day length in Elverum, Norway, where Dæhlie was born, is around five hours and forty minutes.

A: Lake Placid (1932, 1980)

Who Are the Top 10 Individual American Summer Olympians?

Q: Who was Team USA's leading scorer at the 1992 Olympics in Barcelona ("Dream Team")?

1. Michael Phelps
2. Carl Lewis
3. Jackie Joyner-Kersee
4. Jesse Owens
5. Katie Ledecky
6. Misty May-Treanor and
   Kerri Walsh Jennings
7. Simone Biles
8. Mark Spitz
9. Greg Louganis
10. Allyson Felix

You don't need us to tell you that Michael Phelps is the most dominant athlete in the history of any individual sport. My favorite of the endless statistics that illustrate that dominance is: There are no other two Olympians in history who combined to win as many Gold Medals as Phelps did alone. Let us, instead, in the space allotted here, enjoy a glance at the ten-thousand-calorie diet Phelps said he ate each day of the Beijing games in 2008, as reported by Olympics.com.

> *For breakfast, he had three fried egg sandwiches, with cheese, tomatoes, lettuce, fried onions and mayonnaise, followed by three chocolate-chip pancakes ... followed by a five-egg omelet, three sugar-coated slices of French toast, a bowl of grits, and two cups of coffee. ... For lunch, he would have [a] half-kilogram of pasta, two large ham and cheese sandwiches on white bread smothered with mayonnaise, and another set of energy drinks. For dinner, add a pound of pasta with carbonara sauce, a large pizza, and energy drinks.*

Despite this preposterous consumption, Phelps had just 8 percent body fat, burning one thousand calories per hour in the pool. "Eat, sleep, and swim," Phelps told NBC, "that's all I can do."

 A: Charles Barkley (18.0 PPG)

50

What Is the Men's NCAA Tournament All-Time Team?

Q: What is the only school to have a national championship vacated in Division I men's basketball?

1st Team

G Oscar Robertson (1958–60 Cincinnati)
G Gail Goodrich (1963–65 UCLA)
F Christian Laettner (1989–92 Duke)
F Elvin Hayes (1966–68 Houston)
C Lew Alcindor (1967–69 UCLA)

2nd Team

G Magic Johnson (1978–79 Michigan State)
G Jerry West (1958–60 West Virginia)
F Bill Bradley (1963–65 Princeton)
F Danny Manning (1985–88 Kansas)
C Bill Walton (1972–74 UCLA)

3rd Team

G Jay Williams (2000–02 Duke)
G Austin Carr (1969–71 Notre Dame)
F Glen Rice (1986–89 Michigan)
F Jerry Lucas (1960–62 Ohio State)
C Bill Russell (1955–56 San Francisco)

Perhaps the most challenging decision of this entire book was where to place Bill Walton on this list. Candidly, if we were to simply rank the greatest players, he would probably deserve to be second. So to relegate him to the second team hurt me to my core. But fair is fair. He was a center, and to fudge things and place him at a different position on the first team would render the entire exercise invalid. That said, his numbers in the tournament were simply ridiculous. He was eligible to play in three seasons, made the Final Four in all three, and won two national titles. He averaged 21 points and 15 rebounds per game. He scored 29 and had 18 boards in the only game he lost.

And, on March 26, 1973, in the title game against Memphis, he delivered what has to be the tourney's best ever performance: 44 points on 21/22 shooting with 13 rebounds. It has long been my belief that had Walton's body not broken down, he would today be remembered among the handful of greatest players in NBA history. On the college level, that legacy is secure.

A: Louisville (2013)

51

Who Are the Top 10 March Madness Cinderellas?

Q: What is the only school to reach the national title game twice as a 5 seed or lower?

1. 1983 NC State (6 seed)
2. 1985 Villanova (8 seed)
3. 2018 UMBC (16 seed)
4. 2018 Loyola Chicago (11 seed)
5. 2008 Davidson (10 seed)

6. 2011 Butler (8 seed)
7. 1996 Princeton (13 seed)
8. 1987 Providence (6 seed)
9. 1986 LSU (11 seed)
10. 2001 Hampton (15 seed)

At the beginning of April 1983, two exciting things happened. The first was that my family got a VCR. (If you are under the age of fifty, VCRs are what we had before DVDs. If you are under the age of forty, DVDs are what we had before TiVo. If you are under the age of thirty, TiVo is what we used to call DVRs. And if you are under the age of twenty, DVRs are what we had before everything that you ever wanted to watch was available at all times on a streaming service.) Anyway, I was fifteen years old, and I was very excited. Which brings us to the second exciting thing: the NCAA Tournament Finals, featuring an upstart underdog vs. a high-flying powerhouse, NC State against the Houston Cougars, better known as Phi Slama Jama. It would be the first thing we ever taped on our new VCR. I watched a thousand times that wild, victorious coach run around the court, looking for someone to hug. Turned out that coach was from New York, like me—I decided I would root for him from then on. His name, of course, was Jim Valvano. Like many, I practically have that speech committed to memory; I genuinely believe it is the greatest speech ever given in the milieu of sports. Hundreds of millions of dollars have been raised for cancer research because of that speech, and there are people alive who wouldn't have been without it. And it all started with that one game, that one midcourt heave, that sports prayer that didn't go unanswered.

 A: Butler (5 seed in 2010, 8 seed in 2011)

Who Are the Top 10 Most Legendary Division I College Basketball Coaches?

Q: John Wooden coached four (eventual) Hall of Fame players at UCLA—Gail Goodrich, Lew Alcindor, Bill Walton, and whom?

1. John Wooden

2. Pat Summitt

3. Mike Krzyzewski

4. Geno Auriemma

5. Bob Knight

6. Dean Smith

7. John Thompson

8. Tara VanDerveer

9. Rick Pitino

10. C. Vivian Stringer

Separating Wooden and Summitt was among the most difficult decisions we had to make, as their accomplishments, viewed through the prism of history, had vastly different meanings. Pat Summitt built a program—and practically an entire sport—from scratch through her determination, perseverance, and the force of her personality. When viewed as such, Wooden's achievements do not compare. However, viewed differently, one might say that if the objective of a coach is to win championships, Wooden did so at a rate no one had ever imagined. Over the final twelve years of his tenure at UCLA, his team won ten National Championships, including four perfect seasons, and won 335 games while losing just 22. Further, his Pyramid of Success revolutionized not only the ways in which we view coaching, but leadership itself. He implored us all to make each day our masterpiece. He reminded us to be quick, but not hurry. He created a standard for the men's game that has not been approached and never will be. As a coach, he is the standard to which the rest will aspire as long as the game is played.

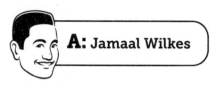
A: Jamaal Wilkes

53

Who Are the Top 10 Most Dominant Champions in Women's College Basketball History?

Q: Who is UConn's three-time Women's Naismith Award winner (most outstanding player)?

1. 2015–16 UConn (38–0)

2. 2001–02 UConn (39–0)

3. 2009–10 UConn (39–0)

4. 2014–15 UConn (38–1)

5. 2013–14 UConn (40–0)

6. 1994–95 UConn (35–0)

7. 1997–98 Tennessee (39–0)

8. 2008–09 UConn (39–0)

9. 2011–12 Baylor (40–0)

10. 1985–86 Texas (34–0)

All that really needs to be known about the dominance of the program built by Geno Auriemma in Storrs, Connecticut, is illustrated by its occupancy of seven of the top eight slots on this list. UConn changed the sport dramatically during that time, elevating it, but also—you may recall—leading some to question whether their dominance was actually bad for the sport. One of the best interviews we ever did on the *Mike and Mike* show was with Auriemma on the morning after the Huskies won the 2010 NCAA Championship. I asked the coach about the idea that his team was hurting the sport by being too good for everyone else. Candid as ever, Auriemma said it was a valid concern. "But," he told us, "the solution is not us getting worse, it's everyone else catching up." Of course, he was not only right but he was also prescient; the sport has never been more popular, and the quality of play has never been higher.

 A: Breanna Stewart (2014, 2015, 2016)

54

Who Are the Top 10 Freshmen in the One-and-Done Era (i.e. Since 2005–06)?

Q: Kevin Durant scored 903 points in 2006–07, a Big 12 single-season scoring record broken by which player?

1. Kevin Durant (2006–07 Texas)
2. Anthony Davis (2011–12 Kentucky)
3. Zion Williamson (2018–19 Duke)
4. Michael Beasley (2007–08 Kansas State)
5. Kevin Love (2007–08 UCLA)
6. Trae Young (2017–18 Oklahoma)
7. Derrick Rose (2007–08 Memphis)
8. Greg Oden (2006–07 Ohio State)
9. John Wall (2009–10 Kentucky)
10. De'Aaron Fox (2016–17 Kentucky)

Kevin Durant was the second-highest-rated player in his high school class, behind big man Greg Oden. Durant said publicly at the time that he would have gone straight to the league from high school if it were allowed, in part because his favorite team, the Raptors, had the first pick. In his one season at Texas, Durant averaged 26 points and 11 rebounds per game and swept all eleven widely known awards for player of the year, including the AP College Player of the Year, the John R. Wooden Award, and the Naismith College Player of the Year. He was the first freshman ever to win any of them. The Longhorns were upset in the second round of the NCAA Tournament by USC despite 30 points and 9 boards from KD. Oden's Ohio State team, meanwhile, made the NCAA Finals, setting the stage for the big man to go number one in the draft—it was still a league about size at that time.

 A: Buddy Hield (925 points in 2015–16)

55

What Are the Top 10 Iconic Calls in Sports Broadcasting History?

Q: Who was Al Michaels's ABC broadcast partner for the "Miracle on Ice"?

1. "Do you believe in miracles? Yes!" —Al Michaels (February 22, 1980)
2. "Down goes Frazier!" —Howard Cosell (January 22, 1973)
3. "The Giants win the pennant!" —Russ Hodges (October 3, 1951)
4. "Havlicek stole the ball!" —Johnny Most (April 15, 1965)
5. "Behind the bag. It gets through Buckner!" —Vin Scully (October 25, 1986)
6. "In your life have you seen anything like that?!" —Verne Lundquist (April 10, 2005)
7. "I don't believe what I just saw!" —Jack Buck (October 15, 1988)
8. "Here comes Willis!" —Marv Albert (May 8, 1970)
9. "The band is out on the field!" —Joe Starkey (November 20, 1982)
10. "Send it in, Jerome!" —Bill Raftery (January 25, 1988)

Honestly, you could put any of these at the top of the list and get almost no argument from me. (With the exception of Bill Raftery's exclamation; it makes the list mostly because a quarter century later it still tickles me every time I hear it.) You might think the "Miracle" call takes the highest place here because of the magnitude of the event but the truth is that the more you think about it, the more critical the actual choice of words becomes. Consider for a moment just how perfectly Al Michaels encapsulated that moment. The game is forever known as "The Miracle on Ice" and the major motion picture it inspired is also called *Miracle*. Are we certain either of those would be the case if Al had shouted "No one thought it possible!" or "The impossible dream has come true!" The perfect call can not only become synonymous with an event, but in fact become an indelible piece of the moment it described.

A: Ken Dryden

56

What Are the Top 10 Stuart Scott Catchphrases?

Q: Who was the leading scorer in the 1982 national title game between Georgetown and Scott's alma mater, North Carolina?

1. "Boo-yah!"
2. "Cool as the other side of the pillow."
3. "He must be the bus driver, cuz he was takin' him to school."
4. "You ain't got to go home, but you got to get the heck up outta here."
5. "Just call him butter, cuz he's on a roll."
6. "Call him carwash, cuz he's automatic."
7. "They call him the Windex Man, cuz he's always cleaning the glass."
8. "It's your world, kid. The rest of us just payin' rent."
9. "Can I get a witness from the congregation?"
10. "That must be jam, cuz jelly doesn't shake like that."

This was a fun list to compile, and the truth is we could have put practically any of them at the top, just as easily as we could have added ten more phrases to the list. I am asked about Stuart all the time; even all these years after his passing he remains perhaps the most beloved ESPN'er ever. What I can tell you is that he was a force of nature: When he walked into a room you felt his presence, and you also darn sure *heard* it. Stuart was filled with energy, bursting at the seams, even when he was sick. He loved working at ESPN, loved what he did, and he made it fun to be there whenever he was in the building. My favorite story about Stuart took place the week of the Super Bowl in Tampa in 2001. My daughter, Nikki, was just four months old, and Stacy was in her final week of maternity leave, so the two of them came down to Florida with me. One afternoon, as we were walking through the lobby of our hotel, I heard my friend's distinctive voice: "Oh, I gotta get some of that!" Stuart was a "girl dad" before that was a term, and his daughters, Taelor and Sydney, are a few years older than Nikki is. They weren't on the trip, and their dad was missing them, so he took baby Nikki and hugged and squeezed and cuddled her the way only a father who misses his babies can. Thankfully, someone took a picture of it. Years later, when Stuart died, we had that picture framed, and it will be on the wall of our home forever. Stuart was terrific; if you'd known him up close, you'd have loved him even more than you already do.

 A: James Worthy (28 points)

57

What Are the Top 8 Yogiisms?

Q: Yogi Berra is one of two catchers in MLB history to win three MVPs (1951, 1954, 1955). Who is the other?

1. "It ain't over 'til it's over."
2. "It's like déjà vu all over again."
3. "When you come to a fork in the road, take it."
4. "Baseball is ninety percent mental, the other half is physical."
5. "It gets late early out there."
6. "Nobody goes there anymore, it's too crowded."
7. "You better cut the pizza in four pieces because I'm not hungry enough to eat six."
8. "I didn't really say everything I said."

As fabulously entertaining as Yogi Berra's malapropisms are, there has always been a part of me that worried they obscured his greatness, both as a player and as a man. Happily, the two can easily be demonstrated with few words. As a ballplayer, Berra was as accomplished as just about anyone that ever lived, an 18-time all-star and 10-time World Series champion, he won three MVPs and was named to the sport's all-century team. Of greater importance, Berra served in the US Navy and, as a second-class seaman, participated in the landings at Normandy as part of a six-man crew, firing machine guns and launching rockets at the German defenses on Omaha Beach. During the battle known as Operation Dragoon, he was shot in the hand and later received several commendations for his bravery. So the next time you chuckle at some of the confusing things the man said, remember you are laughing along with one of the greatest players in the history of baseball and a true American hero.

 A: Roy Campanella (1951, 1953, 1955)

58

Who Are the Top 10 Most Beloved Baseball Broadcasters?

Q: Vin Scully's first game as Dodgers broadcaster was Opening Day 1950. Who was their starting pitcher that day?

1. Vin Scully
2. Harry Caray
3. Mel Allen
4. Bob Uecker
5. Jack Buck
6. Joe Garagiola
7. Red Barber
8. Ernie Harwell
9. Phil Rizzuto
10. Harry Kalas

There are no areas of broadcasting, inside or outside of sports, that create the level of intimacy enjoyed by baseball fans and their favorite team's announcer. The truly great ones, those who stay around a long time, become like members of the family, folks you have spent good days and bad with, through sunshine and rain delays, through the pinnacles of victory and the dourest disappointments of defeat. I believe Vin Scully belongs on the top of any such list, owing to his iconic eloquence and unmatched longevity, but the truth is, your answer to this question depends on which team you love. For me, two of these names especially stand out. As the son of two Bronx-born sports fans, If you ask me what baseball sounds like, I will say that to me it sounds like Phil Rizzuto's voice. Then, when I turned eighteen, I went off to college far away from home, in the suburbs of Chicago. I didn't know a soul when I arrived, but what I quickly learned was that every day the Cubs would play an afternoon game (this was before there were lights installed at Wrigley Field) and the announcer was the most entertaining voice I had ever heard. It didn't matter whether I cared about the Cubs or not. Harry Caray was the first friend I made in Chicago. I will always regret that I never had the chance to tell him all that he meant to me.

A: Don Newcombe

59

What Are the Top 15 Most Hilarious Baseball Names from the 19th Century?

Q: Who is the only player in MLB history to collect 3,000 hits before 1900?

1. Ice Box Chamberlain
2. Cannonball Titcomb
3. The Only Nolan
4. Phenomenal Smith
5. Buttercup Dickerson
6. Peek-A-Boo Veach
7. Oyster Burns
8. Old Hoss Radbourn
9. Foghorn Bradley
10. Live Oak Taylor
11. Boileryard Clarke
12. Jack Glasscock
13. Count Sensenderfer
14. Icicle Reeder
15. Socks Seybold

 few fun notes on these fabulous and fun characters:

- Ice Box Chamberlain, a pitcher, finished 264 of the 301 games he started.
- Cannonball Titcomb's mother was named Fanny.
- The Only Nolan became a police officer in Paterson, New Jersey, after his baseball career was over.
- Phenomenal Smith was credited with discovering the iconic pitcher Christy Mathewson.
- Buttercup Dickerson was inducted into the Italian American Sports Hall of Fame in 1979, despite his granddaughter's insistence that there was no Italian ancestry in the family.
- Old Hoss Radbourn is known for being the first person ever photographed gesturing the middle finger, in 1886.
- Jack Glasscock was the defensive whiz of his era: the first shortstop to lead the league in fielding percentage and total chances in three different seasons—a mark not broken until Ozzie Smith some 85 years later.

 A: Cap Anson (July 16, 1897)

60

What Are the Top 10 Sports Talk Topics of the Last Thirty Years?

Q: Barry Bonds had ten seasons with 20+ home runs and 20+ stolen bases, tied with which player for the most such seasons in MLB history?

1. Should PED users be in the Hall of Fame?
2. Michael Jordan vs. LeBron James
3. Should Pete Rose be in the Hall of Fame?
4. Spygate/Deflategate
5. Instant Replay
6. Expansion of College Football Playoff
7. MLB's Unwritten Rules
8. Brett Favre's Annual Retirement Rumors
9. Peyton Manning vs. Tom Brady
10. Wardrobe Malfunction

The top three on this list could appear in practically any order and get little pushback from me, and it is worth noting that there was most certainly a time when Rose's name would have topped this list without debate. But time passes, and important things happen. And the steroid scandal in baseball—misunderstood as it will always be—marks both an end point and new beginning to the recorded history of the sport. There is no measurement of the game's offensive statistics that is not hopelessly skewed by its effect. Lest there be any confusion, the simple fact is this: In the nearly 150-year history of MLB, there have been six instances of a player hitting 63 or more home runs in a season, and they *all* came in a four-season span, from 1998 through 2001. This isn't complex to decipher, and the sport has paid a severe price: The most revered records in its history have been rendered forever meaningless. Such is life. Thus, I offer no apologies for the endless hours Mike and I spent debating, dissecting, and defining the issues after José Canseco's 2005 book broke open the dam of information on this subject. In the end, steroids impacted baseball in ways most sports have never been affected by anything. The topic was well worth every breath of air it consumed.

A: Bobby Bonds

61

What Are the Top 10 Most Impactful Rule Changes in Sports?

Q: Who led the NBA in 3-pointers from 2018–20 during his streak of three consecutive scoring titles?

1. NBA institutes 3-point line in 1979

2. MLB institutes live ball in 1920

3. NHL institutes "icing" rule in 1937

4. NFL introduces instant replay in 1986

5. MLB moves mound back from 50' to 60'6" (1893) and lowers mound from 15" to 10" (1969)

6. NBA institutes shot clock in 1954

7. American League institutes designated hitter in 1973

8. NFL institutes overtime for regular-season games in 1974

9. NBA institutes Wilt Chamberlain–necessitated rule changes (widening lane, offensive goaltending, inbounding-ball revisions, free-throw revisions)

10. College basketball permits dunking in 1976

For well over a century, these games we love to watch people play have all repeatedly undergone major renovations for various reasons ranging from business to safety to competitive fairness. However, the top three on this list stand well above the rest due to the monumental impact they had in their respective sports. There was baseball before the live ball and then baseball after, but those two are *not* the same thing and should never be confused as such. Likewise for hockey and icing, and for the NBA and the three-point line. In all candor, we placed the basketball on top based sheerly on recency bias, which is to say I actually remember what the sport was like without it. And I'm not positive it wasn't better. I know that's a controversial opinion, but I come by it honestly. I learned it the same way I learned everything else: from observing my father sitting in our living room, carrying on like a "first time, long time" caller to a radio show. "Michael," I can still hear him complain, "the objective of the game is supposed to be to pass the ball around until you get the best possible shot, as close as you can to the basket, not as far away." He didn't live to see what Steph Curry has become to the league, and to our culture, and I often wonder if he would have adapted his thinking. What Steph does is inarguably beautiful, and the way his teams have always valued sharing the ball, and outstanding passing does harken back to the game's earliest days. I think my father would have liked the Warriors, though I'm not sure they would have changed his mind about the three-point shot. Either way, what is certain is that the 3-point goal forever changed the game of basketball, I'll leave it to you to decide if it was for the better or not.

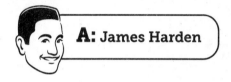

A: James Harden

Who Are the Top 10 Most Influential Team Owners?

Q: Which team waived Jim Plunkett in 1978, allowing the Raiders to sign him as a free agent?

1. Al Davis—Raiders (1966–2011)
2. George Steinbrenner—Yankees (1973–2010)
3. Bill Veeck—Indians (1946–49), Browns (1951–53), White Sox (1959–61, 1975–81)
4. Walter O'Malley—Dodgers (1950–79)
5. George Halas—Bears (1936–82)
6. Ted Turner—Braves (1976–96), Hawks (1977–96)
7. Jerry Jones—Cowboys (1989–Present)
8. Jerry Buss—Lakers (1979–2013)
9. Conn Smythe—Maple Leafs (1927–61)
10. Green Bay Packers, Inc. (1923–Present)

Over the course of my three decades in broadcasting I have had the great thrill and privilege of meeting many of the most important legends in the history of sports. Among them all, none loomed larger in my imagination than the fiery owner of the Oakland Raiders, Al Davis. The man did just about everything a football person can: He was an assistant coach, a head coach, a league commissioner, a general manager, and a team owner. He was a supervillain, an antihero, a renegade, a visionary, and a genius. He hired John Madden and Jon Gruden. He made Art Shell the first African American head coach the league had ever seen, Tom Flores the first Latino head coach, and Amy Trask the first female chief executive. Nine different inductees selected Davis as their presenter at the Pro Football Hall of Fame. His motto "Just Win, Baby" became synonymous with his franchise, and the sport itself.

A: 49ers

Who Are the Top 10 Sports Prodigies?

Q: Which player interrupted Wayne Gretzky's streak of eight consecutive Hart Memorial Trophies by winning MVP in 1988?

1. Wayne Gretzky
2. Tiger Woods
3. Serena Williams
4. LeBron James
5. Michael Phelps

6. Sidney Crosby
7. Ken Griffey Jr.
8. Nadia Comăneci
9. Bob Feller
10. Bryce Harper

Tiger Woods was on *The Mike Douglas Show* when he was three years old. Serena Williams was interviewed by CNN when she was nine. LeBron James was on the cover of *Sports Illustrated* when he was seventeen. Each of the prodigies on our list somehow managed to outperform impossible expectations, and for that alone they deserve to be lauded. But there has never been anything quite like the burden placed on the young Wayne Gretzky. To this day, in his home, he keeps a copy of the newspaper article for which he gave his first interview. He noted, "The headline says, 'Hull, Richard, Howe and Gretzky.' . . . That was lots of pressure." Gretzky was nine years old when that story was written. Such was the magnitude of belief and hope that an entire hockey-mad nation carried for its future favorite son—it would *not* have been enough for him merely to become a Hall of Fame–caliber player. While Tiger, Serena, and LeBron can each legitimately stake a claim to being the greatest in the history of their sports, none of them would have been deemed *failures* had they merely become great; Gretzky absolutely would have. He *had* to be The Great One. He was forecast as the best to ever live before he reached puberty, and hardly a soul in all of Canada didn't know it. The weight of that expectation is difficult to fathom. That he actually managed to do it is a greater achievement than all his statistical records combined.

A: Mario Lemieux

64

Who Are the Top 10 Ahead-of-Their-Time Athletes?

Q: In 1977, Billie Jean King became the second women's tennis player to surpass $1 million in career winnings. Who was the first?

1. Billie Jean King
2. Oscar Robertson
3. Arnold Palmer
4. Michael Vick
5. Martina Navratilova

6. Deion Sanders
7. Joe Namath
8. Tiger Woods
9. Reggie Jackson
10. Nikola Jokić

I love the diversity of this list because there are so many ways in which athletes can be ahead of their time. In the case of The Big O, before he played basketball it was a very compartmentalized game. Some players were scorers, others rebounders, others distributors, and very rarely were players asked—or able—to do more than one. Robertson averaged a triple-double over his first *five* NBA seasons, decades before the term was so much as considered. Others, like Palmer, Namath, and Jackson put the "super" in superstars. By and large, sports stars had seldom become true national celebrities in the way that movie stars and musicians had. These three changed all of that. Among my earliest memories: Palmer on a tractor, Namath in pantyhose, Jackson's first name on a popular candy bar. The athletes of today who earn millions of dollars in endorsements owe a debt of gratitude to the pitchmen who paved their path. Still, in all of sports history there has never been anyone like Billie Jean King. Long before her Battle of the Sexes victory over Bobby Riggs, and seemingly every day since, she did and has done as much to further the cause of equality for all as any athlete in our nation's history. There will be other trailblazers, inside and outside the world of sports, but there will never be another Billie Jean King.

A: Chris Evert (1976)

Who Was the Best Player Drafted with Each Pick, 1–14, since the NBA Lottery Era Began in 1985?

Q: LeBron James is one of two No. 1 overall picks to make his NBA debut at the age of 18. Who is the other?

1. LeBron James (2003)

2. Kevin Durant (2007)

3. James Harden (2009)

4. Chris Paul (2005)

5. Scottie Pippen (1987)

6. Damian Lillard (2012)

7. Stephen Curry (2009)

8. Ron Harper (1986)

9. Dirk Nowitzki (1998)

10. Paul Pierce (1998)

11. Reggie Miller (1987)

12. Mookie Blaylock (1989)

13. Kobe Bryant (1996)

14. Tim Hardaway (1989)

What is most interesting about this list, I think, is the least-interesting players. Choosing among immortals is one thing, thus are LeBron, KD, and Kobe easy choices, as they would be on any list. Some of the other names that fill out this roster, however, will likely surprise you as much as they did us. Ron Harper had a noteworthy career, starring on excellent Cleveland teams before winning titles alongside Michael in Chicago. But for his to be the most significant career in a top-ten slot illustrates just how top-heavy the NBA Draft can be. (By way of irrelevant comparison, among the NFL stars drafted eighth overall are Ronnie Lott, Lance Alworth, and Christian McCaffrey.) Further, Mookie Blaylock is better remembered for his collegiate career than his thirteen seasons in the NBA, where he made one all-star team and twice led the league in steals, but he is still quite easily the most accomplished player drafted in his spot.

A: Dwight Howard

66

What Were the Worst 5 No. 1 Overall Picks in the NBA Draft?

Q: Los Angeles is the third city in which the Clippers franchise has played. What were the first two?

1. Michael Olowokandi (1998)
2. Markelle Fultz (2017)
3. Greg Oden (2007)
4. Kwame Brown (2001)
5. Anthony Bennett (2013)

When assessing the abject awfulness of a draft selection, it is imperative to consider the options that were available to the team at the time. Thus, while the meager accomplishments of Anthony Bennett perhaps might seem to warrant greater skepticism than some of the others, the criticism of that pick is tempered slightly by the fact that the best player selected close behind him was Victor Oladipo. (A scrawny, virtual unknown from Greece named Giannis went 15th in that class, evidence that absolutely no one in the league foresaw what he might become.) Meanwhile, Greg Oden ahead of Kevin Durant is as devastating as any miss could be, though, giving some latitude here, we'll never know what Oden might have been had he remained healthy. The Markelle Fultz blunder is especially egregious considering the Sixers swapped up to take him, gifting the Celtics the ability to pick Jayson Tatum at a discounted rate. And still, absolutely nothing can match the sheer disaster of the Clippers selecting Olowokandi atop one of the greatest draft classes of all time, one that saw Vince Carter, Dirk Nowitzki, and Paul Pierce all go to other teams in the hour that followed.

 A: Buffalo (1970–78), San Diego (1978–84)

67

What Is Greeny's All-Time Starting Five for the New York Knicks?

Q: Patrick Ewing made his last All-NBA team in 1997. Who was the next Knicks player to make one?

PG Walt Frazier
SG Earl Monroe
SF Bernard King
PF Willis Reed
C Patrick Ewing

When I was growing up, the NBA was not nearly as popular as it is today. Such was its comparative obscurity that, in those days, my friends and I would arrive at Madison Square Garden five minutes before tip-off of practically every Knicks home game and purchase tickets to sit in the "blue" seats, traditionally known as "the nosebleeds." The tickets cost six dollars, but if you produced proof that you were a student, you got them at 50 percent off. Then we would spend the entire first quarter scouting out seats right behind the bench, of which plenty were always empty. After the first quarter was over, the ushers wouldn't chase us away when we snuck down. Ergo, we spent practically our entire adolescence in the best seats in the house for three dollars apiece. (Those same behind-the-bench seats are selling for $1,028 apiece on StubHub.) I say all this to establish my credentials as a knowledgeable fan of the franchise and its history. Meaning, if you try to come at me with Carmelo Anthony over Bernard King, I am ready for you. King played only three seasons for New York, but I am here to say they were the best seasons any Knicks player ever had. This is particularly true for the 1983–84 season, in which King scored 50 points in back-to-back games, made first team All-NBA, and averaged 35 points per game in two thrilling playoff series. To me, it isn't especially close. Melo was terrific, but Bernard was the King.

 A: Amar'e Stoudemire (2011)

What Are 10 Things Greeny Misses about Sports that Are Never Coming Back?

Q: Whose death did Howard Cosell announce to a *Monday Night Football* audience on December 8, 1980?

1. Howard Cosell's voice
2. Stadiums not named after products
3. A pitching duel involving only two pitchers
4. Hockey players without helmets
5. Football hits that hurt just watching them
6. World Series day games
7. Stickum
8. Home team wearing white
9. Barefoot kickers
10. Three to make two

I struggled mightily choosing between the top two here, as the days when you knew where a game was being played simply by saying the name of the venue were positively delightful. If you are my age, you will go to your grave knowing where Candlestick Park, the Forum, and Three Rivers Stadium were. I defy anyone to tell me in which city you might find Bank of America Stadium, Nissan Stadium, or the Frost Center. Of course, I miss everything on this list. But none of them as much as Howard. When you heard his voice, you felt as if you were in the center of the universe because he brought you with him. There are still big game announcers today, sure. But none who feel bigger than the game itself. He was a star in a way no one in the role has ever been since. Here's what I mean: When Cosell did highlights at halftime of *Monday Night Football*, he didn't do every game; he only did the important ones. That meant that through my entire childhood, he never once mentioned the Jets. Then, one night, it happened. It was 1981, and the Jets were mounting a late-season push toward the playoffs. And Cosell included their game amid the usual flurry of Steelers, Raiders, and Cowboys. I went racing from my room, shouting at the top of my lungs: "Dad, you're not going to believe this! Howard Cosell knows who the Jets are!"

A: John Lennon's

What Are the Top 10 Iconic Hockey Goals?

Q: Who is the only defenseman to win more Hart Memorial Trophies (MVP) than Bobby Orr's three?

1. Bobby Orr's flying goal (May 10, 1970)

2. Mike Eruzione's game-winner in "Miracle on Ice" (February 22, 1980)

3. Paul Henderson's "Goal of the Century" (September 28, 1972)

4. Alex Ovechkin scores "The Goal" from his back (January 16, 2006)

5. Sidney Crosby's golden goal (February 28, 2010)

6. Patrick Kane's Stanley Cup winner (June 9, 2010)

7. Bill Barilko's Stanley Cup winner (April 21, 1951)

8. Ron Hextall scores first true goalie goal (December 8, 1987)

9. Mario Lemieux's "What a goal! What a move!" (May 17, 1991)

10. Stéphane Matteau's "Matteau Matteau Matteau!" (May 27, 1994)

There is no substitute for being at the right place at the right time. And, on May 10, 1970, forty seconds into overtime of a Stanley Cup Final game at Boston Garden, Ray Lussier certainly was. Lussier was positioned in precisely the perfect spot, camera at the ready, when Bobby Orr scored the goal that won the Bruins the cup and then proceeded to leap into the air in a manner befitting the superhero he was. Lussier captured what is absolutely the most iconic moment in NHL history. It was the first championship for the Boston team in 29 years, and the goal was scored by the greatest, and most beloved, player in franchise history. When Orr's number was retired in Boston, nine years after the night of the legendary "Flying Goal," the fans rewarded him with a standing ovation that lasted eleven minutes. Ray Lussier died too young, but the photograph he took on that magical night will live as long as the game of hockey is played.

A: Eddie Shore (4)

Who Are the Top 10 Enforcers in NHL History?

Q: What are the names of the three brothers that played the role of enforcers for the Charlestown Chiefs in the movie *Slap Shot*?

1. Tiger Williams
2. Bob Probert (half of the "Bruise Brothers")
3. Terry "Bloody" O'Reilly
4. Tie Domi
5. Marty McSorley
6. Dave "The Hammer" Schultz
7. Eddie Shore
8. Rob Ray
9. Stu "The Grim Reaper" Grimson
10. Donald Brashear

Dave "Tiger" Williams had a more than respectable NHL career: A second-round draft choice in 1974, he played in fourteen seasons for five different teams, earning one all-star game appearance and appearing in the 1982 Stanley Cup Final with Vancouver. However, when you google his name, the first stats about him that pop up tell the story you really need to know.

Tiger Williams's National Hockey League records:

Most NHL career regular-season penalty minutes: 3,971

Most NHL penalty minutes, career, including playoffs: 4,426

So prolific was Williams at accumulating time in the penalty box that his record for minutes is over 500 more than the next person in the record books: Dale Hunter—this despite Hunter having played five more seasons and over 400 more games. During the Canucks' run to the Cup Final in 1982, Williams was at his combative best, setting records for most penalty minutes in a series and a playoff year. (He amassed 116 penalty minutes in 17 postseason games.) It feels worth mentioning that Williams had seven seasons in which he tallied 40 or more points, including two in which he scored 30 or more goals. But, again, it is the penalty box that will always be known as this Tiger's natural habitat.

A: Jeff, Steve, and Jack Hanson

71

Who Have the Top 10 Biggest Slap Shots in NHL History?

Q: Bobby Hull recorded five 50-goal seasons with the Blackhawks. Who is the only other player in franchise history with more than one such season?

1. Bobby Hull
2. Al MacInnis
3. Al Iafrate
4. Bernie "Boom Boom" Geoffrion
5. Zdeno Chára
6. Brett Hull
7. Ray Bourque
8. Shea Weber
9. Alex Ovechkin
10. Chris Chelios

If one were to judge purely based on numbers, MacInnis would deserve the crown. After all, he won the NHL's hardest shot competition seven times, the most in history. MacInnis had a shot so hard that he once delayed the start of a game by putting a puck *through* the boards behind the net in warmups. However, MacInnis didn't change the game—Bobby Hull did. While none of Hull's slap shots were ever measured, legend holds that at least once he reached 118 mph—this in a time when the game was played with wooden sticks, before the advent of composite graphite sticks made everyone's shots harder. Hull's shot was fast enough that he caused the league to legislate the curvature of the stick. Starting in 1965, Hull began experimenting with larger curvatures of the blade, leading goalies across the league to complain it created an unfair advantage. Toward the end of the decade the NHL would limit the curvature to three-quarters of an inch, and then in 1970 to no greater than one-half inch. Considering this, alongside Hull's standing as arguably among the dozen greatest players in history, earns him the top curved blade on this list.

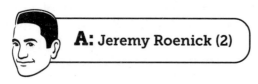

A: Jeremy Roenick (2)

72

Who Had the Top 10 Rookie Seasons in NHL History?

Q: Which NHL franchise has produced the most Calder Memorial Trophy (Rookie of the Year) winners?

1. 1992–93 Teemu Selänne

2. 1979–80 Wayne Gretzky
(played 1978–79 season
in WHA)

3. 1969–70 Tony Esposito

4. 2005–06 Alex Ovechkin

5. 1950–51 Terry Sawchuk

6. 1980–81 Peter Šťastný

7. 1986–87 Ron Hextall

8. 1979–80 Ray Bourque

9. 1985–86 Patrick Roy

10. 1977–78 Mike Bossy

By the time the man forever known as The Finnish Flash arrived in the NHL, he was already an accomplished star in his native country, having led the professional league, Liiga, in scoring. He was 22 years old when he got to Winnipeg, where he put together the greatest rookie season the sport had ever seen; his 76 goals and 132 points remain NHL rookie records, and he was an easy choice for the Calder Memorial Trophy as the top first-year player in the league. Selänne honed his athletic skills as a youth competing against his twin brother, Paavo, who went on to become a member of multiple European championship teams in field hockey. The ice is where Teemu excelled, eventually becoming the highest-scoring Finnish player in NHL history, surpassing his childhood idol, Jari Kurri, and following Kurri as the second Finn elected to the Hockey Hall of Fame. But all that came at the end of his twenty-one-year career. It was the beginning, that first year, for which Selänne remains best remembered, still the greatest rookie season in the history of the sport.

 A: Toronto Maple Leafs (10)

73

What Have Been the Top 10 Most Influential NHL Captaincies?

Q: Who succeeded Mark Messier as Rangers captain after his retirement in 2004?

1. Mark Messier, Oilers (1989–91) and Rangers (1992–97, 2001–04)
2. Jean Béliveau, Canadiens (1962–71)
3. Steve Yzerman, Red Wings (1987–2006)
4. Denis Potvin, Islanders (1980–87)
5. Scott Stevens, Devils (1993–2004)
6. Joe Sakic, Avalanche (1991, 1993–2009)
7. Jonathan Toews, Blackhawks (2009–present)
8. George Armstrong, Maple Leafs (1958–69)
9. Bobby Clarke, Flyers (1973–79, 1983–84)
10. Ray Bourque, Bruins (1986–2000)

What Mark Messier put together in 1989–90 is one of the most improbable, overlooked, and brilliant years in the history of the sport. Messier captained Edmonton to its fourth Stanley Cup in six years just two seasons after it traded away the greatest player that ever lived at the very apex of his popularity and prowess. Without Wayne Gretzky to lead the way, Messier did, winning the Hart Memorial Trophy as the league's MVP. Better remembered, of course, is the cup Messier won in New York, captaining the Rangers to their first championship in 54 years, still their only title season since 1940. Down three games to two in the conference finals, Messier guaranteed a win, then scored a natural hat trick in the third period. He also scored the game-winning goal in game seven of the finals, becoming the first—and still only—player ever to captain two different franchises to Stanley Cup championships. In 2006, the NHL created the Mark Messier Leadership Award, given to an individual in the sport who leads by example and motivates his teammates—the ultimate tribute to the ultimate captain, as great a leader as the game has ever seen.

A: Jaromír Jágr

74

What Are Greeny's 10 Favorite Sports Movies (Drama)?

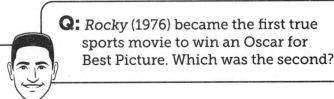

Q: *Rocky* (1976) became the first true sports movie to win an Oscar for Best Picture. Which was the second?

1. *Rocky*   **6.** *Victory*

2. *Remember the Titans*   **7.** *Heaven Can Wait*

3. *Hoosiers*   **8.** *A League of Their Own*

4. *Raging Bull*   **9.** *Breaking Away*

5. *Jerry Maguire*   **10.** *Brian's Song*

It has been my experience doing sports talk that the subject of sports movies is among the most passionate and divisive topics we have. As such, it felt necessary to separate the humorous takes from the serious; let's face it, *Raging Bull* and *Kingpin* have no more in common than orange sherbet and goose liver pâté. In the category of sports drama, I select *Rocky* amongst a crowded field of contenders. The characters in that film are what sets it apart for me—every one of them indelible, each one perfectly cast. Apollo Creed, Mickey, Paulie, Adrian—each one more iconic than the next. The film also features perhaps the most important usage of theme music in the history of the screen—"Gonna Fly Now" may be the best known song in movie history and the one most directly associated with its film. (When we interviewed Stallone on *Mike and Mike,* he told us the "score," as he called it, was what won the film the Oscar.) Finally, the real-life underdog story of how the movie came to be made—in which Stallone is every bit as unlikely a champion as the character he created—is irresistible. Among this group of heavyweight films, you really couldn't go wrong. But for me, *Rocky* is the champ.

 A: *Chariots of Fire* **(1981)**

75

What Are Greeny's 10 Favorite Sports Movies (Comedy)?

Q: Who blew a three-shot lead on the 18th hole at the 1999 Open Championship?

1. *Caddyshack*
2. *Bad News Bears*
3. *Slap Shot*
4. *Kingpin*
5. *Major League*
6. *Tin Cup*
7. *Dodgeball: A True Underdog Story*
8. *Happy Gilmore*
9. *Bull Durham*
10. *Fast Break*

This category was much easier for me. While I love all the comedies on this list, there has never been a movie—in any genre—I enjoy more than I do *Caddyshack*. That was true in the summer of 1980, when my parents took me to see it in the theater, and it remains so to this day. In fact, I would argue the film holds up better than most of its era, perhaps because the country-club culture it lampoons has hardly changed a bit in the four decades since the movie released. The better debate, actually, is which of the four legendary leads is the funniest in the movie: Chevy Chase, Bill Murray, Rodney Dangerfield, or Ted Knight. (I think I would choose Knight, but could probably be talked into any of them if you catch me on the right day.) Finally, a fun story. In 2004, I did a feature for ABC's coverage of golf's Western Open called "Whatever happened to Danny Noonan?" I brought the actor, Michael O'Keefe, to the driving range at a tour event to shoot it, and what I found was that PGA Tour stars reacted to him the way I'd imagine they would to Bobby Jones if he came back to life. The moral of that story was simple: Everyone who loves golf loves *Caddyshack*.

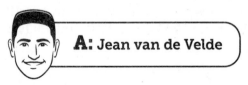

A: Jean van de Velde

76

Who Are the Top 10 Most Iconic Racehorses of All Time?

Q: Which horse extinguished the longest drought between Triple Crown winners in history?

1. Secretariat
2. Man o' War
3. Citation
4. Seattle Slew
5. Affirmed

6. Dr. Fager
7. American Pharoah
8. Zenyatta
9. Kelso
10. Seabiscuit

It is very hard to quantify such a thing, particularly when talking about a horse, but I do think an argument could be made that Secretariat was the greatest athlete of the twentieth century. You already know all the accomplishments, particularly winning the Triple Crown in 1973, setting records in all three races that still stand. But the true measure of an athlete can never be made in numbers or records alone. There is an element of magic, an air of superiority—an "it" factor—that is necessary to set the truly special ones apart. It was Seth Hancock, whose family established the legendary breeding operation Claiborne Farm in Kentucky, where Secretariat is buried, who made the case best: "You want to know who Secretariat is in human terms? Just imagine the greatest athlete in the world. The greatest. Now make him six foot three, the perfect height. Make him real intelligent and kind. And on top of that, make him the best-lookin' guy ever to come down the pike. He was all those things as a horse."

A: American Pharoah (2015, 37-year drought)

77

Who Are the Top 5 Legendary Pro Wrestlers?

Q: Who was Dwayne "The Rock" Johnson's head coach during his football career at the University of Miami?

1. The Rock

2. Hulk Hogan

3. Andre the Giant

4. Ric Flair

5. Bruno Sammartino

In my youth, pro wrestling was my ultimate guilty pleasure. My brother and I loved to watch what was then known as *Georgia Championship Wrestling* on TBS on Saturday evenings, with Gordon Solie as the host. *GCW* eventually morphed into *WCW*, while WWF was growing and expanding, and before I knew it, wrestling was no longer a sneaky escape but rather a major entertainment entity. Rowdy Roddy Piper and Jimmy "Superfly" Snuka gave way to Ric Flair, Andre the Giant, and Hulk Hogan, each of whom became mainstream stars in ways no wrestlers before had ever imagined, appearing in major Hollywood motion pictures, attracting attention and audiences well beyond the squared circle. But not even in *their* wildest imagination could they have smelled what The Rock was cooking. Dwayne Johnson may very well be the biggest star in all of entertainment; as of this writing he has 395 million followers on Instagram, making his the fifth-most-followed account on planet Earth. The sport—if that is indeed the appropriate word—has come an awfully long way from the days of Bruno Sammartino, who deserves his place on this list as the first true star of the ring.

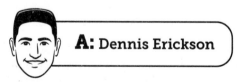

A: Dennis Erickson

What Are the Top 10 Auto Racing Families?

Q: The winner of which race drinks milk in Victory Lane, a tradition that dates to the 1930s?

1. Andretti (Mario, Michael, John, Jeff, Marco)
2. Petty (Lee, Richard, Kyle, Adam)
3. Earnhardt (Ralph, Dale Sr., Kerry, Dale Jr., Jeffrey)
4. Unser (Louis, Bobby, Al Sr., Johnny, Al Jr.)
5. Allison (Bobby, Donnie, Davey, Clifford)
6. Mears (Roger, Rick, Casey)
7. Jarrett (Ned, Glenn, Dale)
8. Labonte (Terry, Bobby, Justin)
9. Busch (Kurt and Kyle)
10. Baker (Buck, Buddy, Randy)

*T*he *Guinness Book of World Records* calls Mario Andretti "the most versatile driver" in the history of auto racing, attributing that title to the four different seasons in which he won races on paved ovals, road courses, and dirt tracks. The accolades Andretti earned over the course of a five-decade career made him one of the few true mainstream celebrities the sport would produce; as a boy growing up in the 1970s in New York, the only two drivers I knew (because everyone did) were Andretti and Richard Petty. Mario Andretti was born in an Italian territory that is today part of Croatia, and with his family fled his native land after World War II and spent seven years in a refugee camp. Andretti began racing on dirt tracks in Pennsylvania in 1959, at the age of 19. By the time he was finished, he would compete in 879 races and win 111. He and A. J. Foyt remain the only drivers ever to win both the Indianapolis 500 and the Daytona 500, and in 2000 the Associated Press named Mario Andretti the Driver of the Century.

A: Indianapolis 500

79

What Are the Top 10 Officiating Blunders?

Q: What was the first country to defeat the United States men's basketball team by double figures in the Olympics?

1. 1972 Olympic Men's Basketball Final (September 9, 1972)

2. Diego Maradona's "Hand of God" goal (June 22, 1986)

3. "The Call" by Don Denkinger (October 26, 1985)

4. Roy Jones Jr. robbed of Olympic gold (October 2, 1988)

5. Rams–Saints no-call (January 20, 2019)

6. Brett Hull's skate in the crease (June 19, 1999)

7. The Imperfect Game (June 2, 2010)

8. Jeffrey Maier home run (October 9, 1996)

9. Fifth Down Game (October 6, 1990)

10. George Brett's pine tar home run (June 24, 1983)

If you ask practically anyone who watched the 1972 US Men's Olympic basketball team "lose" to the Soviet Union in the finals, they won't say this game was decided by a "blunder," but rather that the gold medal was stolen from the American team. You already know about the three times the final three seconds of the game were played, the result being the first time America ever lost an Olympic basketball game. Doug Collins has always been among the most vocal of those players; he sank two free throws after being knocked nearly unconscious with three seconds remaining, two points that should have won the game. Instead, Doug lived with pain and regret, and without the silver medal he and his teammates declined to accept. Then a wonderful thing happened. Doug's son, Chris, now the head coach at Northwestern, earned a gold medal as an assistant for the 2008 Redeem Team. (Actually, a replica; coaches do not receive actual medals.) Giving that medal as a gift to his father was, as Chris describes it, "the proudest day of my life." At least one of those players got his Olympic gold.

A: Puerto Rico (92–73 in 2004)

80

Who Had the Top 10 Sports Rants of All Time?

Q: Which player held the distinction as shortest NBA MVP before Allen Iverson (listed at 6–0) won the award in 2001?

1. Allen Iverson ("Practice?")
2. Herm Edwards ("You play to win the game!")
3. John McEnroe ("You cannot be serious!")
4. Jim Mora ("Playoffs?!")
5. Dennis Green ("They are who we thought they were!")
6. Mike Gundy ("I'm a man, I'm forty!")
7. Bart Scott ("Can't wait!")
8. Richard Sherman to Erin Andrews ("Don't you ever talk about me!")
9. Mike Tyson on Lennox Lewis ("I want to eat his children!")
10. Lee Elia ("Print it!")

May 7, 2002. I was a young, aspiring *SportsCenter* anchor with a side hustle at ESPN Radio on a morning show that I figured might last three years if I was lucky. I was anchoring the evening edition of *SportsCenter* alongside Chris McKendry; none of us working on the show that night could have possibly known what we were in for. Allen Iverson was, at the time, the most controversial star in the NBA: brilliantly talented, mercurial, and tough as nails. Iverson's relationship with his equally brilliant and equally difficult coach, Larry Brown, had reached a boiling point. *That* story would take far more space than we have here—suffice it to say we had enough of a sense that Iverson might say something pointed after the Sixers' lost in the first round to the Celtics that we went live to the press conference he held after the game. And . . . we got much more than we bargained for. In response to critics who felt he should do more in practice, Iverson mockingly said the word *practice* twenty-two times with increasing disdain. He said plenty of other words too, many that are spelled with four letters. Let the record show that when the press conference ended, and we came back live to the studio, it was me who apologized for the language the audience had heard. As I recall, it was all I could do to get even those few words out. Like everyone else, Chris and I were dumbstruck by the raw emotion Iverson displayed that day. Candidly, it was something of a perfect distillation of the man himself: honest, vulnerable, combative, human. That rant will never be forgotten, and neither will the greatness of the player who spoke it.

 A: Bob Cousy (listed at 6–1)

81

Who Are the Top 10 If-Not-for-Injury Athletes?

Q: Who is the only player in Auburn history with more career rushing touchdowns than Bo Jackson's 43?

1. Bo Jackson
2. Tiger Woods
3. Maureen Connelly
4. Bill Walton
5. Sandy Koufax
6. Grant Hill
7. Monica Seles
8. Derrick Rose
9. Tony Conigliaro
10. Eric Lindros

When I first met Bo, he was already damaged goods. He was playing for the White Sox, it was 1993, and Vincent Edward Jackson was a shell of himself. The artificial hip, the avascular necrosis—I can't imagine what it must have been like for him. Bo Jackson was the greatest athlete I ever saw. His athletic gifts belong in a tiny room of sports history alongside Wilt Chamberlain, Jim Brown, Deion Sanders—the all-time great two-sport athletes of our nation's history. The young Bo was a brilliant baseball player—had he played a full career he'd almost certainly have been a perennial all-star. But, it was in football where he almost certainly would have become an immortal. The Heisman Trophy in 1985, the first pick in the draft that followed, the combination of power and speed that—at most—a handful of running backs ever possessed, before or since. Playing only part-time, Bo averaged 6.8 yards per carry as a rookie. No one who watched it will ever forget him exploding through Brian Bosworth on *Monday Night Football*. I genuinely believe that had Bo Jackson been healthy and played a full NFL career he would today be remembered as one of the greatest running backs in the history of the sport, alongside Brown, Walter Payton, and Barry Sanders. He was the great miss of his time, sadly, and maybe of any time.

 A: Carnell "Cadillac" Williams (45)

82

Who Are Greeny's Top 10 Athletes of the '70s Who Deserve to Be Better Remembered Today?

Q: Which MLB, NBA, NFL, or NHL team won the most championships during the decade of the 1970s?

1. Ann Meyers

2. Lee Trevino

3. Chuck Foreman

4. Dave Cowens

5. Steve Garvey

6. Guillermo Vilas

7. Olga Korbut

8. Harold Carmichael

9. Graig Nettles

10. George McGinnis

There are few trailblazers in sports history less remembered than Ann Meyers. Upon occasion, she is somewhat frivolously recalled as the first woman to sign a contract with an NBA team, which she did with the Pacers in 1979. She participated in three-day tryouts with the team, the first woman ever to do so with any team, and while she never played, she did become one of Indiana's broadcast analysts long before many women were working in that capacity. You may have known that much about Ann's career—but there is so much more. In 1975, Meyers became the first high school player ever to make the roster of a US National Team, after which she became the first female athlete ever to receive a four-year athletic scholarship from any university. Meyers starred at UCLA, becoming the first four-time All-American in the history of the women's game. In 1978, Meyers recorded the first quadruple-double in NCAA Division I history; only four others have accomplished it since, one male and three female. In 1990, Meyers's jersey (#15) was one of the first four retired by UCLA in a ceremony at Pauley Pavilion, along with Denise Curry (#12), Kareem Abdul-Jabbar (#33), and Bill Walton (#32). In 2007, Meyers was enshrined in the FIBA Hall of Fame as part of the inaugural class, one of three American players so honored, alongside Bill Russell and Dean Smith. If reading all of this causes your jaw to drop, my point is made.

A: Montreal Canadiens (6)

Who Are the Top 10 Major-Sport Athletes to Never Win a Title?

Q: Who played the most games for the Giants since the team moved to San Francisco in 1958?

1. Barry Bonds
2. Ty Cobb
3. Ted Williams
4. Barry Sanders
5. Dan Marino
6. Anthony Muñoz
7. Karl Malone
8. Marcel Dionne
9. Charles Barkley
10. Ernie Banks

Please be aware, if it galls you to see the names Bonds and Cobb above Ted Williams, I share your disgust. Williams was an American hero, serving our nation during two different wars, and perhaps the greatest pure hitter the game has ever seen. Meanwhile, the name directly above his on this list is every bit as associated with bigotry and violence as it is baseball, and the one at the very top most certainly used methods that were against the rules—and the law—to transform himself from a merely great player to the most unstoppable offensive force of all time. Such is the lot in life of baseball history in the post-steroid era; there is nothing more challenging than trying to put into perspective that which cannot be quantified. All I have to base a decision on is what is directly in front of us, and that is that Barry Bonds hit more home runs than any player who ever lived, he won seven MVP awards—three of which came before his hat size "magically" increased—and that in the one World Series he played in, he hit four home runs and walked 13 times in seven games, finishing the series with an on-base percentage of .700 while slugging 1.294. Those are video-game numbers, and Bonds was a cheat code, literally and figuratively. He belongs at the top of this list, even if down deep you wish he didn't.

 A: Willie McCovey (2,256)

84

What Are the Top 10 Major-Sports Teams That Didn't Win a Title?

Q: Which Giants player sacked Tom Brady twice in Super Bowl XLII?

1. 2007 Patriots
2. 2015–16 Warriors
3. 1906 Cubs
4. 1942 Bears
5. 2001 Mariners
6. 1970–71 Bruins
7. 1968 Colts
8. 1972–73 Celtics
9. 1995–96 Red Wings
10. 1998 Vikings

The 2007 season began amid controversy for the New England Patriots. Their opening game was against the Jets, coached by Eric Mangini, a former Pats assistant, who reported that his old team was using equipment to record the Jets' signals from across the field. The "Spygate" controversy that ensued cast a shadow over the entire Patriots organization. Don Shula, the winningest coach in NFL history, said, "The Spygate thing has diminished what they've accomplished. You would hate to have that attached to your accomplishments. They've got it. . . . I guess you got the same thing as putting an asterisk by Barry Bonds's home run record." Tedy Bruschi, a linebacker for the Patriots at the time, has said that all the doubt fueled his team's subsequent pursuit of perfection. The Patriots didn't want to merely defeat their opponents, they wanted to humiliate them, in part to prove they were as good as advertised, with no need of illegal assistance. Their regular season was something to behold. In no game did they score fewer than 20 points, scoring over 40 four times and over 50 twice. Heck, they *averaged* 41 PPG for their first ten games. The way that season ended will, of course, never be forgotten. David Tyree's miracle helmet catch earned the Giants an improbable championship in Super Bowl XLII—and it cost the Patriots something even greater. Had they won, there is no doubt that the 2007 Patriots would be remembered as the greatest football team of the modern era.

A: Justin Tuck

85

What Are the Top 10 Actual Baseball Team Names?

Q: On which minor-league team did Joe DiMaggio hit safely in 61 consecutive games in 1933?

1. Augusta GreenJackets
2. Lansing Lugnuts
3. Rocket City Trash Pandas
4. Akron RubberDucks
5. Vallejo Seaweed

6. Amarillo Sod Poodles
7. Toledo Mud Hens
8. Austin Weirdos
9. Dublin Leprechauns
10. Santa Fe Fuego

To be clear, not only are these all real team names, they are teams for which real stars have played. Madison Bumgarner pitched for the Augusta GreenJackets in 2008. The website of the Lugnuts boasts that roughly 20 percent of their all-time roster appeared in major-league games, including Carlos Beltran, who spent time in Lansing in 1996. Torey Lovullo managed the RubberDucks in 2005. Every great baseball story has a beginning, and many of them begin on teams with hilarious names.

 A: San Francisco Seals
(Pacific Coast League)

86

What Are Hembo's Top 10 Most Distinguished Ballparks?

Q: Which player hit the most career home runs at Wrigley Field?

1. Wrigley Field
2. Fenway Park
3. Polo Grounds
4. Ebbets Field
5. Yankee Stadium

6. Rickwood Field
7. Camden Yards
8. Shibe Park
9. Hinchliffe Stadium
10. Sportsman's Park

I remember it like it was yesterday—June 20, 2014. A friend and I were driving across the Midwest on a baseball road trip as a last hurrah before I moved to Connecticut to begin my career at ESPN. On that day, we visited Wrigley Field for the first time. The concourse was crowded and dingy, but nobody seemed to mind. It smelled and sounded like a different century. (I am a sucker for organ music.) That rich ivy looked like it stretched for miles. And when I laid eyes on it, I had an epiphany: On that 81-degree Friday afternoon, I was about to watch baseball be played in its natural habitat. Where Ernie Banks played two. Where Babe Ruth called his shot. Where the creatures bleacher. Where the seventh inning stretches. Where the losers are loved, though that day the Cubs won. The Cubs entered the day 31–40, but 36,421 others still showed up with us to watch.

A: Sammy Sosa (293)

87

What Are the Top 5 Most Bizarre Concessions at a Baseball Game?

Q: Ichiro Suzuki batted .300 in 10 Gold Glove seasons, tied with which player for most in MLB history?

1. Slider Dog—hot dog with macaroni and cheese, bacon, and Froot Loops (Guardians)
2. Cleanup Burger—four patties on waffles, hash browns, egg, cheese, bacon (Braves)
3. Yard Dog—three foot-long hot dogs covered in crab dip and Old Bay potato sticks (Orioles)
4. Burgerizza—twenty-ounce cheeseburger with two pepperoni pizzas as buns (Braves)
5. Pork Mac and Cheese Cone—waffle cone filled with pork, coleslaw, macaroni and cheese, and barbecue sauce (Guardians)

What is there to say?

A: Roberto Clemente

What Are the Top 10 Games in NFL History?

Q: Who is the only QB to beat Don Shula (as a head coach) multiple times in the playoffs?

1. The Guarantee | Super Bowl III (1968)
2. The Greatest Game Ever Played | 1958 NFL Championship
3. The Helmet Catch | Super Bowl XLII (2007)
4. The Ice Bowl | 1967 NFL Championship
5. 28–3 | Super Bowl LI (2016)
6. The Immaculate Reception | 1972 AFC Divisional
7. The Catch | 1981 NFC Championship
8. The Drive | 1986 AFC Championship
9. Epic in Miami | 1981 AFC Divisional
10. 13 Seconds | 2021 AFC Divisional

The Super Bowl has become, without close competition, the most important annual event on our national calendar. Nothing brings more people together, no spectacle is more extraordinary, no cultural event more scrutinized, analyzed, or monetized. In the modern era, the pageantry has extended well beyond the traditional parameters of sport, with people who have never watched a football game still partaking earnestly, whether they be invested in the pricey commercials, the halftime entertainment, or simply enjoying the company of a raucous gathering of family and friends. Had it not been for Joe Namath and his legendary guarantee, and the most important upset in the history of sports, it all may very well have never been. The first two "AFL-NFL Championship Games" were dominated by the Green Bay Packers, so much so it left columnists and fans alike to wonder whether there was any reason for the annual match to continue. Curt Gowdy, who broadcast the game, said, "Pete Rozelle told me there was anxiety that if there were another lopsided game, they'd have to scrap the game or create a new formula for it." The point had been made: The AFL teams simply did not belong on the field with the traditional NFL powerhouses. Paul Maguire, the legendary broadcaster whose career began as a linebacker and punter for the Chargers and Bills, would tell me decades later: "When the Jets won, it was like all of us in the AFL won." The truth is, everybody won that day. As Namath ran off that field in Miami, with one finger pointed toward the sky, he ushered in the modern era of pro football.

 A: Jim Kelly (1990, 1992, 1995)

89

Who Are the Top 10 Most Intimidating Defenders in NFL History?

Q: Which (eventual) Hall of Fame coach served as Bears defensive coordinator in Dick Butkus's rookie season (1965)?

1. Dick Butkus
2. Lawrence Taylor
3. Mean Joe Greene
4. Jack Tatum
5. Mike Singletary

6. Ray Nitschke
7. Deacon Jones
8. Ronnie Lott
9. Jack Lambert
10. Chuck Bednarik

We lost the great Dick Butkus just before I sat to write this chapter, and thus the ferocious images of his highlights are rather fresh in my mind—to the very end, he left every one of us in awe. In the long, storied, and glorious history of professional football, there has been no legend greater, no name more revered, and certainly no man more feared. That last one is hardly hyperbole: Mike Ditka is the roughest, toughest, meanest sonofagun I have ever known personally. I have known him for half my life, and in all those years I have only ever heard him acknowledge being intimidated by one man. That man was Butkus—in *practice*. The two were teammates, so Butkus scared the hell out of Iron Mike in *practice*. There isn't room here for as many Butkus stories as I would love to tell, but among my favorite notes: He weighed thirteen pounds, six ounces at birth; the Bears went 1–13 in 1969, with Butkus racking up 25 tackles in that one victory; a Lions running back named Altie Taylor once called Butkus "overrated," so the next time the teams met Butkus chased Taylor so far out of bounds after a play that the running back leaped into the stands to get away. The stories go on; the legend will only continue to grow. Dick Butkus, rest in peace, or in whatever form of mayhem you might prefer.

A: George Allen

90

What Are the Top 10 Super Bowl Halftime Shows?

Q: Which stadium has hosted the most Super Bowls?

1. Michael Jackson (Super Bowl XXVII)
2. Prince (Super Bowl XLI)
3. Beyoncé and Destiny's Child (Super Bowl XLVII)
4. Bruno Mars and the Red Hot Chili Peppers (Super Bowl XLVIII)
5. U2 (Super Bowl XXXVI)
6. Dr. Dre, Snoop Dogg, Eminem, Mary J. Blige, and Kendrick Lamar (Super Bowl LVI)
7. Jennifer Lopez and Shakira (Super Bowl LIV)
8. Tom Petty and the Heartbreakers (Super Bowl XLII)
9. Diana Ross (Super Bowl XXX)
10. Janet Jackson, Justin Timberlake, P. Diddy, Kid Rock, and Nelly (Super Bowl XXXVIII)

I watched the sun set over the mountains in the distance from my seat in the Rose Bowl's auxiliary media section. As Garth Brooks finished singing the national anthem, military jets flew overhead in formation. As the crowd roared in unison, I felt tears welling in my eyes. I thought of all the Super Bowls I had watched throughout my life. How I had dreamed of someday being there. And now that dream had come true. The moment was surreal and emotional for me, and remained fully that way long after the Dallas Cowboys and Buffalo Bills took the field and the day became about a football game once again. I had just about recovered my composure when the game went to halftime. And then, my breath was taken away. Michael Jackson created the first true "must-see" halftime in the history of the event, and in every conceivable way it was most certainly that. Troy Aikman was named the MVP. But the unquestioned star of the show was Michael Jackson.

 A: Superdome (New Orleans)

Who Were the Top 10 Favorite Athletes of Greeny's Childhood?

Q: Which QB owns the record for most career touchdown passes in the AFL?

1. Joe Namath
2. Chris Evert
3. Walt Frazier
4. Thurman Munson
5. Joe Klecko

6. Sugar Ray Leonard
7. Julius Erving
8. Earl Monroe
9. Reggie Jackson
10. Pete Rose

My mother hates when I make this joke, but I sometimes wonder if that is because, like most good jokes, there is the tiniest kernel of truth in it. At countless events over the years, many of them with Joe in attendance, I have said that my mother would have left my father for Joe Namath, and my father would have applauded her for it. In the home in which I was raised, Namath was not merely an athlete, he was practically a deity. Charismatic, audacious, charming, clever, and cool as all hell, Joe was the first football superstar in the modern sense of the word. The leader of the only Jets team ever to win a championship could do no wrong for us, no matter the ups and downs of his life after football. I am delighted to report that as of this writing, Joe is as healthy and sharp as I've ever known him to be, and he and I have developed a friendship that means everything to me. By the way, after my father died in January of 2016, Joe asked me to bring my mother to a golf event the following fall, which I did. Joe saw to it that she was seated beside him, and they chatted and laughed all evening long. It was the happiest I saw her that year. The only thing better than meeting your idols is when they turn out to be even better people than you imagined. There will only ever be one Broadway Joe.

A: Len Dawson (182)

What Are the Top 10 Wish-I-Had-Been-There-in-Person Sporting Events?

Q: Jackie Robinson played all 151 games of his 1947 rookie season for the Dodgers at which position?

1. Jackie Robinson breaks color barrier (April 15, 1947)
2. Jesse Owens at 1936 Olympics
3. Miracle on Ice (February 22, 1980)
4. Fight of the Century (Ali-Frazier I on March 8, 1971)
5. Don Larsen's perfect game (October 8, 1956)
6. Battle of the Sexes (Billie Jean King defeats Bobby Riggs on September 20, 1973)
7. Wilt Chamberlain's 100-point game (March 2, 1962)
8. Lou Gehrig's "Luckiest Man" speech (July 4, 1939)
9. Christian Laettner hits "The Shot" (March 28, 1992)
10. Bobby Thomson's "Shot Heard Round the World" (October 3, 1951)

From a pure sporting perspective, there are any number of ways one could approach this question. But when one steps back and considers the magnitude of each event, there is only one correct answer. Jackie Robinson changed all of America one afternoon at Ebbets Field in Brooklyn in front of 26,623 spectators, more than 14,000 of whom were Black. The day Robinson broke the color barrier belongs on the short list of the most important days in twentieth-century America, right alongside the day Neil Armstrong set foot on the moon. Robinson's grace, humanity, and athletic genius have been documented in more books than perhaps any athlete who ever lived. There have been many days that sports fans will never forget. There has never been one as important as the one authored by Jackie Robinson, and there never will be again.

 A: First base (moved to 2B in 1948)

Who Are the Top 10 Starters I Want Pitching with My Season on the Line?

Q: Who was the losing pitcher in both of Sandy Koufax's World Series shutouts?

1. Sandy Koufax
2. Bob Gibson
3. Christy Mathewson
4. Curt Schilling
5. Whitey Ford

6. Madison Bumgarner
7. John Smoltz
8. Catfish Hunter
9. Josh Beckett
10. Andy Pettitte

It is reasonable to wonder about Sandy Koufax; if he hadn't suffered injuries so debilitating that he was forced to retire at the age of thirty, would he be regarded today as the greatest pitcher who ever lived? During his career, he was certainly the most dominant. Koufax was the first to win the Cy Young Award three times, each of them on unanimous votes, and remains the only pitcher to do so when a single award was given for both leagues. He led the National League in ERA each of the last five seasons of his career; in three of those his ERA was under 2.00. Further, if you look at his statistics in the most important games of his career, you realize he always rose to the occasion, even though his teammates frequently did not. Koufax started seven World Series games and never allowed more than two earned runs in any of them. His World Series ERA was 0.95, and yet his record was a mere 4–3 due to an almost total lack of run support. In those seven starts, Koufax threw four complete games, two shutouts, and struck out 60 batters in 55 innings. There have been a lot of big-game pitchers, to be sure, and it is worth noting that if we had included relievers in the category then Mariano Rivera would almost certainly have topped the list. But when baseball was at its best, it was because you gave a pitcher the ball and hoped never to take it back. Given that scenario, if I was managing, I would give the ball to Koufax.

A: Jim Kaat (Games 5 and 7 in 1965)

94

Who Are the Top 10 Should-Be Baseball Hall of Famers That Were Better Than You Remember?

Q: In 1972, Dick Allen became the second player in White Sox history to win an MVP. Who was the first?

1. Dick Allen
2. Johan Santana
3. Lou Whitaker
4. Bret Saberhagen
5. Kenny Lofton

6. Keith Hernandez
7. Bobby Grich
8. David Cone
9. Graig Nettles
10. Luis Tiant

There may be no Hall of Fame candidacy more confounding than that of Richard Anthony Allen. Goose Gossage described him as "the greatest player I've ever seen play in my life." In 1977, Oakland Athletics owner Charlie O. Finley said of Allen: "I wouldn't touch him with a ten-foot pole." Finley signed him eight days later. Statistically, Allen has a strong case as baseball's greatest non–Hall of Famer not connected to performance-enhancing drugs. In an 11-season span from 1964–74, he produced the best batting line in baseball (165 OPS+); Willie McCovey ranked second (161). During that time, his 68.5 offensive WAR led the majors; Hank Aaron ranked second (63.9). And yet, Allen topped out at 18.9 percent of the Hall of Fame vote on the writers' ballot (75 percent needed for induction) and fell one vote shy during the Golden Days Era Committee voting in 2014 and 2021. "I was labeled an outlaw," Allen wrote in his memoir. "And after a while that's what I became."

A: Nellie Fox (1959)

95

Who Are the Top 10 "One-Hit Wonders"?

Q: Who knocked out Mike Tyson in the last heavyweight title fight of his career?

1. Buster Douglas
2. David Tyree
3. Bucky Dent
4. Y. E. Yang
5. Roberta Vinci

6. Don Larsen
7. Mark Fidrych
8. Ickey Woods
9. Timmy Smith
10. Johnny Vander Meer

In all my years loving sports, which means all the years of my life, there has probably never been an utterance that surprised me more than Jim Lampley's "Say it now, gentlemen, James Buster Douglas—undisputed heavyweight champion of the world!" To say Buster Douglas was an underdog would be like saying The Rock looks like he's done a few curls. Douglas was 42–1 against Mike Tyson that night in Tokyo; when Cassius Clay "shook up the world" by knocking out Sonny Liston the odds were 7 to 1. So the improbable nature of the one hit for Douglas is what separates him on this list. Tyree's catch, Dent's home run, even Yang chasing down Tiger, all those were less shocking than the image of Tyson on the canvas groping for his mouthpiece. Thereafter, Douglas's fade from the pinnacle of the sport was practically immediate; he was fifteen pounds overweight for his first title defense, in which he was knocked out in the third round by Evander Holyfield. Over the next several years, his weight ballooned to nearly 400 pounds and he nearly lost his life to diabetes. Ultimately he did attempt what proved to be a short-lived comeback, but, in the end, what cannot be disputed is that Buster Douglas had his moment in the sun, one that will never be forgotten by anyone who saw it.

A: Lennox Lewis (2002)

96

What Are the Top 10 MVP Snubs of All Time?

Q: By total points, who is the leading scorer in NBA history to never win an MVP?

1. 1961–62 Wilt Chamberlain
2. 1987 Jerry Rice
3. 2000 Pedro Martínez
4. 1985 Dwight Gooden
5. 1996–97 Michael Jordan

6. 1942 Ted Williams
7. 2006–07 Martin Brodeur
8. 1982 Dan Fouts
9. 1962 Willie Mays
10. 2005–06 Kobe Bryant

In 1961–62, Wilt Chamberlain put together the greatest season in the history of the NBA. That is not an opinion; it is an obvious fact. Where do we begin? I suppose on March 2, the night Chamberlain scored 100 points in Hershey, Pennsylvania. For the season, he averaged 50.4 points and 25.7 rebounds per game; the 4,029 points he scored remain the most in NBA history, and the only time any player eclipsed the 4,000-point mark. (The closest anyone else ever came was Michael Jordan, who scored 3,041 in 1986–87, 25 percent *fewer* points than Wilt.) Wilt also averaged 48.53 minutes per game—multiple overtimes enabled him to average more than the regulation 48. (In all, he played 3,882 of his team's 3,890 minutes, only missing those 8 minutes due to an ejection.) Chamberlain was named the first team all-NBA center that season, ahead of Bill Russell, but it was Russell who was named the season MVP.

A: Carmelo Anthony (28,289 points)

97

What Are the Top 10 Most Lopsided Trades of All Time?

Q: Babe Ruth played his final season in 1935, for which team?

1. 1919—Yankees acquire Babe Ruth from Red Sox for $100,000
2. 1996—Lakers acquire Kobe Bryant from Hornets for Vlade Divac
3. 1989—Cowboys acquire 5 players and 8 draft picks (used to acquire Emmitt Smith, Darren Woodson, Russell Maryland, and Kevin Smith) from Vikings for Herschel Walker and 4 draft picks (all 3rd round or later)
4. 1900—Giants acquire Christy Mathewson from Reds for Amos Rusie
5. 1980—Celtics acquire Robert Parish and No. 3 pick (Kevin McHale) from Warriors for No. 1 pick (Joe Barry Carroll) and No. 13 pick (Rickey Brown)
6. 1965—Orioles acquire Frank Robinson for Milt Pappas, Jack Baldschun, and Dick Simpson
7. 2022—Seahawks acquire Charles Cross, Boye Mafe, 5th-round pick (traded), Devon Witherspoon, Derick Hall, Noah Fant, Shelby Harris, and Drew Lock from the Broncos for Russell Wilson and a 4th-round pick
8. 1976—76ers acquire Julius Erving from Nets for $3 million
9. 1965—76ers acquire Wilt Chamberlain from Warriors for Paul Neumann, Connie Dierking, Lee Shaffer, and $75,000 cash
10. 1992—Packers acquire Brett Favre from Falcons for 1st-round pick (used to draft Tony Smith)

Babe Ruth was sold to the Yankees in order to finance a Broadway play that you have never heard of. I can think of no better example to demonstrate just how different a place sports occupy in our society than they did a century ago. Contrary to popular myth, Ruth was *not* sold to finance the popular *No, No, Nanette*, which has had multiple runs on Broadway and spawned the classic song "Tea for Two." Ruth was actually sold in order to secure financing for the little-seen play *My Lady Friends*, which itself spawned a silent movie of the same name in 1921. *No, No, Nanette* was subsequently based on *My Lady Friends*—all of which is a long way to reiterate: *The greatest star baseball ever saw was sold to finance a play!* For perspective, Ruth was already a household name; he had been the American League home run leader each of the preceding two seasons in Boston, while still performing as a starting pitcher, and Boston had just won the 1918 World Series. As you are no doubt aware, because of the Curse of the Bambino, the trade meant Boston would not win another for 86 years. Meanwhile, Ruth (as goes without saying) redefined what athletic stardom could mean and became the greatest legend in the history of American sport. There have always been, and will always be, bad trades, but there will certainly never be anything quite like this again.

A: Boston Braves

98

What Are the Top 10 Most Impactful Trades in NHL History?

Q: What was the only NHL team to acquire Wayne Gretzky via free agency?

1. Wayne Gretzky from Oilers to Kings (1988)
2. Eric Lindros to Flyers, Peter Forsberg to Nordiques (1992)
3. Patrick Roy from Canadiens to Avalanche (1995)
4. Phil Esposito from Black Hawks to Bruins (1967)
5. Mark Messier from Oilers to Rangers (1991)
6. Ken Dryden from Bruins to Canadiens (1964)
7. Ted Lindsay/Glenn Hall from Red Wings to Black Hawks (1957)
8. Ron Grahame from Bruins to Kings for pick that nets Ray Bourque (1978)
9. Brett Hull from Flames to Blues (1988)
10. Dominik Hašek from Blackhawks to Sabres (1992)

The Wayne Gretzky "trade tree" (i.e., how any trade turns out once all the picks and everything else are completed), not unlike the deal itself, was fascinating, impactful, and seemingly everlasting. Some 12,453 days after The Great One was shipped from Edmonton to Los Angeles, the final player to skate for the Kings as a result of the trade left the NHL for the KHL. Fitting that a deal so monumental would remain tangible for more than 34 years. The impact it had in Gretzky's homeland cannot be overstated either. Peter Pocklington, the Edmonton owner who sold off Gretzky for two players, three draft picks, and $15 million in cash, was burned in effigy after the deal was announced. Such was the outrage across Canada that New Democratic Party House Leader Nelson Riis demanded the government block the trade. "Wayne Gretzky is a national symbol like the beaver [...]" he said. "How can we allow the sale of our national symbols?"

 A: New York Rangers (1996)

99

What Are Wayne Gretzky's Top 5 Most Unbreakable NHL Records?

Q: Who is the only player in NHL history with more points as a teenager than Wayne Gretzky's 220?

1. Four 200-point seasons (no other NHL player has one)

2. 163 assists in 1985–86 season (next-most in non-Gretzky season is 114 by Mario Lemieux in 1988–89)

3. 8 consecutive MVPs (Hart Memorial Trophy) from 1980–87 (next-most is 3 straight by Bobby Orr from 1970–72)

4. 575 career multi-assist games (next-most is Mario Lemieux's 282)

5. 382 career points in playoffs (next-most is Mark Messier's 295)

My beloved friend Jalen Rose always used to say to me, "There should be two record books—one for Wilt Chamberlain, and the other for everybody else." And, as usual, he was dead right. Chamberlain recorded numbers that so dwarfed his competition that it became redundant—and thus served to actually diminish the magnitude of his achievements. The same can occasionally be said of Gretzky. Consider: There have been four 200-point seasons in NHL history, and Gretzky recorded them all, in a five-season span between 1982–1986. (He fell only four points short of making it five consecutive 200-point seasons during that time.) Taken a step further: Gretzky recorded nine of the top thirteen scoring seasons in history, while Lemieux had the other four. (Lemieux's highest total was 199 in 1988–89.) As of this writing, the highest total by any player *other* than Gretzky or Lemieux is 155, recorded by Steve Yzerman in 1988–89. In case you need further convincing, I'll finish with this: If in Gretzky's record season he had scored *zero* goals, his total points would *still* have been higher than Yzerman's. Do not let the sheer numbers obscure the greatness—Wayne Gretzky really should have his own record book.

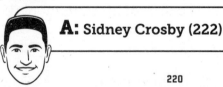

A: Sidney Crosby (222)

100

What Are Wilt Chamberlain's Top 5 Most Unbreakable NBA Scoring Records?

Q: Who was the second-leading scorer in NBA history after Wilt Chamberlain (31,419 points) at the time of his retirement (1973)?

1. 117-game span averaging 50 PPG (no other player in NBA history has averaged 50 PPG in more than any 5-game span)
2. 1,200 made FG in 4 consecutive seasons (next-most in non-Wilt season is 1,159 by Kareem Abdul-Jabbar in 1971–72)
3. 50.4 PPG in 1961–62 season (next-most in non-Wilt season is 37.1 by Michael Jordan in 1986–87)
4. 32 career 60-point games (next-most is 6 by Kobe Bryant)
5. 100 points in game on March 2, 1962 (next-most in game is 81 by Kobe Bryant on January 22, 2006)

Which leads us conveniently back to Chamberlain, and the afore-mentioned mockery he made of the record books during his fourteen NBA seasons. The 117-game streak averaging 50 is almost impossible to comprehend—again drawing my concern that as such it doesn't sink in as much as it should. Let me try to demonstrate this differently. In his career, Chamberlain had 118 games scoring at least 50 points. As of this writing, the players with the next-most such games, in order, are: Michael Jordan, Kobe Bryant, James Harden, Elgin Baylor, and Damian Lillard. If you add together all the times they did it, it comes to 111. The point is, you could choose practically any of Wilt's records and accurately describe them as unbreakable—like Gretzky, it is as though he was playing a different sport from everyone else. Pity the rest; they all don't deserve to be held up to impossible standards.

A: Oscar Robertson (25,822 points)

ACKNOWLEDGMENTS

First off, I would like to thank both the extraordinary team at *Get Up*, and the entire Hashtag Crew from ESPN Radio; it is a privilege to work with all of you every day. Thanks, too, to the crew at CAA, including David Larabell, Mike "Vino" Levine, Tom Young, Marco Critelli, Adam Biren, Jeff Jacobs, and Rob Light. None of this would be possible without Team Greeny: Nick Khan, Mark and Jason Bradburn, Richard Koenigsberg, and Erika Echavarria. And, most of all, endless thanks to every one of you who has chosen to start your day with me over the last 25 years, I hope it has been as much fun for you as it has for me.

—Greeny

Thank you. To my extraordinary wife, Lizzie, for encouraging me to pursue my dreams. To Greg Thompson and Tom Johnstone, for your inspiration, our shared fandom, and friendship. To Greeny, for your daily investment into my career. And to all those who read, listen, and watch, for the unending support.

—Hembo

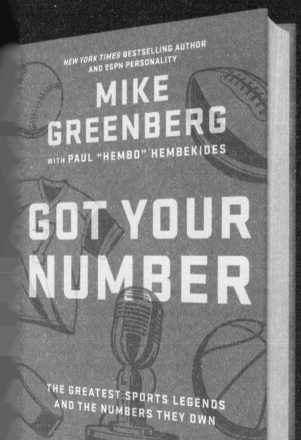

NEW YORK TIMES BESTSELLING AUTHOR
AND ESPN PERSONALITY

MIKE
GREENBERG

with PAUL "HEMBO" HEMBEKIDES

GOT YOUR
NUMBER

THE GREATEST SPORTS LEGENDS
AND THE NUMBERS THEY OWN

ailable wherever books are sold.

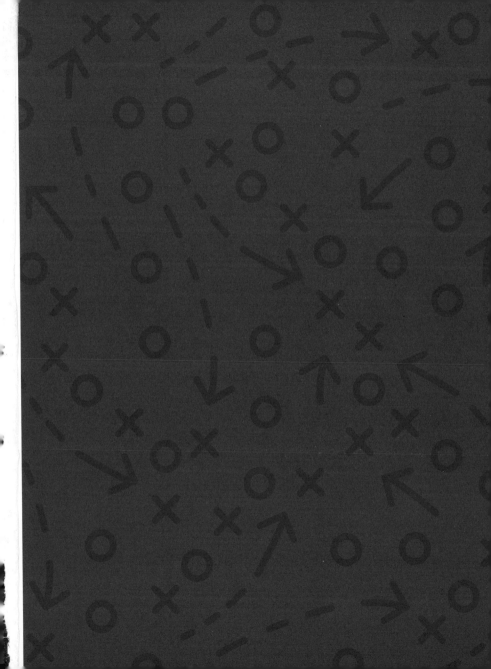

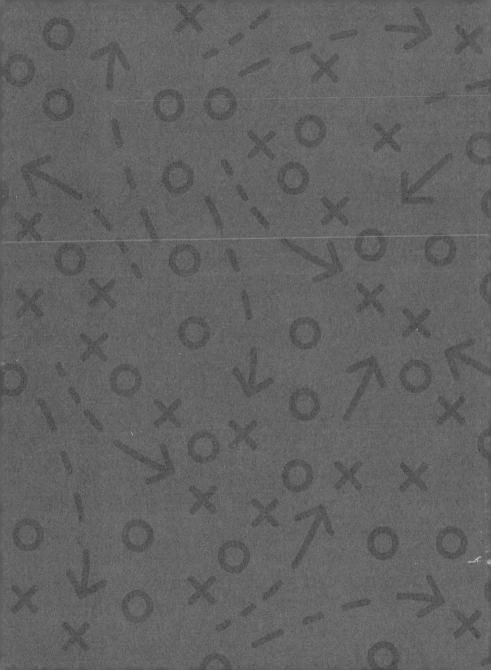